EASTWOOD

Nottinghamshire

Volume Two

Harry Riley

and

Brian Fretwell

All rights reserved. Without limiting the rights

under copyright reserved above

No part of this publication may be reproduced,

stored in or introduced into a retrieval system

or transmitted in any form or by any means

without the prior written permission

of the copyright owner and publisher of this book.

The owner acknowledges the trademarked status

and trademark owners of the various products

referenced in this work which have been used

without permission. The publication / use of these

trademarks is not authorised, associated with

or sponsored by the trademark owners

This 2nd. 'Eastwood digest' is dedicated to Norman (Sol) Davis

Retired 'Moorgreen Pit' miner and 'number one'

Supporter of

The Badgers, (the indomitable Eastwood Town Football Club)

Contents

Table of Contents

Introduction 6
Chapter 1: A town and District Evolves. 8
Chapter 2: Purposeful Lives 46
Chapter 3: A Country Park 59
Chapter 4: Community Stalwarts 64
Chapter 5: Health and Beauty 87
Chapter 6: Friend and Mentor of D. H. Lawrence 92
Chapter 7: Anniversary Archives 119
Chapter 8 'Entertainment' 135
Chapter 9: Sporting, School, Work and Church 155
Chapter 10: Remembering 'Owd Eastwood' 197
Chapter 11 : Civic Duty and Assorted Subjects 222
Chapter 12: Keeping Eastwood's Businesses Growing 258
Chapter 13: More Important Memories 273
Chapter 14: Healthier Living 313

Introduction

In the first volume I asked a rhetorical question:

What is there to say about Eastwood?

Well, the first book was so well received that Brian Fretwell and I felt obliged to offer up a second one, Brian (with his wealth of knowledge, concerning the lives of so many Eastwood folk, and the community in general) doing the legwork/research, and me collating, writing/editing and filling in some of the many omissions from the first book, as feedback from Norman (Sol) Davis, was quick to point out. He quite rightly remarked that nothing had been written about **The Buildings.** Norman has lived there all his life and Eastwood Town grew up around these squares of colliers homes. Norman claims to be the oldest ex-miner still living in the buildings, designed and built in the nineteenth century by the Barber Walker Mining Company.

There will be more from Norman later, as we dip into the major mining influence and The Badgers, sporting story.

So in this second volume, of the social history of Eastwood Nottinghamshire and its surrounding villages and small towns we want to feature more of the colourful and notable sons and daughters, those local folk who have given NG16 its special character.

What is our purpose? Well, neither of us are publishing this book to make money. We are both retired and think it would be a good thing to pass on to future generations, so they might get a feel of life in those early days, and to see how things have progressed. Again we apologize for omissions.

Some of the more personal stories have been set out virtually as the teller describes, others have been edited with as little interference as possible.

I was not born at Eastwood, coming from Aspley, or Aspleh! As one well-known Eastwoodite informs me. So I am still a foreigner, even after thirty years or more of breaking Eastwood bread.

Harry Riley

Chapter 1: A town and District Evolves.

As part of the year 2000 millennium celebrations Michael Bennett of Eastwood Library edited a book on behalf of Eastwood Historical Society, entitled: **A Century Remembered.** Astonishingly it is now 16 years since the publication of this splendid book. It is packed full of the reminiscences, superb photographs and anecdotes from residents of Eastwood and the surrounding district. This is a *must read* for anyone interested in the social history of our town.

Harry Riley's Note: there will be more from Eastwood Historical Society in Vol: 3 for 2017.

With volume two of Eastwood Past and Present we are not attempting to compete, duplicate or emulate the remarkable work of Michael Bennett; that would be too enormous a task to follow, but we will endeavour to put our own slant on things and to show the ongoing work of more of the town's talented sons and daughters and perhaps the founders of some commercial traders who've chosen to make Eastwood their home base.

It appears we have lost Durban House to the savage economic cuts afflicting the county and indeed the whole country, but small mercies, the D.H. Lawrence Birthplace Museum and Breach House are both still being maintained and open for tourists and literature lovers as we write. M.P. Gloria de Piero is fighting a valiant battle to try and save Durban House, but it seems a forlorn hope.

The creators of this book, asked the 'National Trust' if they would consider saving Durban House for the Nation, but apart from an acknowledgement of our letter, it seems the plea has fallen on deaf ears.

However we have to be positive and look on the bright side. Eastwood is still a great place to live and to bring up a family, with all our shopping, health, schooling and recreational facilities near at hand.

Even more importantly the residents themselves are resilient to change and will not be defeated easily. Crime is no worse than in many other areas of Nottinghamshire and our police, fire and ambulance services remain available and intact.

We still have a vibrant Eastwood Library Service that is refreshingly adapting to change, as was discovered during a recent visit, to the sound of a parents and toddlers group having enormous fun, as they joined in the chorus of a well known nursery tune, and filling their lungs, screaming in unison to demonstrate how they'd react on seeing a crocodile. I was half inclined to join 'em.

A bit different to my generation's childhood memories of libraries with 'silence' notices everywhere, in glaring, foot-high text, and with the distinct possibility of being forcibly evicted from the library if we kids' even dared to sneeze too loudly.

So, hopefully the good old, bad old days are now well and truly behind us, but that is not to say we should forget and pretend they never existed.

Eastwood and district is constantly changing and evolving as large industrial sites and buildings close, or undergo a change of use. After some local opposition we now have a thriving retail park including Ikea, down at the bottom of Giltbrook Hill. Like it or loathe it, this has brought jobs and prosperity to the area. Particularly at weekends the car parks are full to bursting, with people arriving from far and wide to shop in one place.

Just around Ikea Island and along the A610 bypass, heading towards Codnor and Ripley is the **Winston wind turbine,** and this structure, over 400 foot high, is another cause of divided opinion, being visible from many directions and for miles around.

In September 2015 Brian Fretwell and I led a 'Chapter and Verse' community group walk from Langley Mill, along the Erewash Valley Trail and via the Nottingham Canal, to view the wind turbine close up.

We called this the 'Winston Wander' and it was part of the Erewash and Amber Valley 'Footprints Festival of 2015.' We led a party of 16 walkers, which included an artist, several photographers, and a great grandmother, with daughter (and grandson in a pushchair,) also two visitors from North Yorkshire, (literature lovers) holidaying at Eastwood to take in the famous D.H. Lawrence Heritage Trails and to soak up the glorious Notts, Derbyshire countryside.

It was a fine day and an opportunity to view Winston close up. Winston being so named, following a competition by Awsworth schoolchildren.

Our walk was labelled as a gentle, four mile stroll, taking in the two local canals: Erewash Canal and Nottingham Canal lagoons, and viewing the wind turbine close up, situated in the middle of a field. We began at Anchor Bridge Langley Mill, just across from the 'Great Northern' Public House.

The turbine was commissioned for 'Severn Trent' Water Treatment Plant. It has steps inside going right to the top and in the gear chamber at the top it is said a man can stand upright to carry out any required maintenance.

Our 'Winston Wander' began and ended at the Erewash Valley Trail, with good dry walking all the way.

The Erewash Valley Trail

The Erewash Valley trail covers over thirty miles of tranquil countryside, abundant wildlife and waterways, where once there were noisy pits and railways.

Winston, glimpsed from the nearby hedgerow

The famous 'Flying Scotsman' brilliantly caught on camera by Paul Kirk as it passed by Winston wind turbine near Shipley Boat and Erewash canal lockside. The train was on route to York and Paul insists it arrived a minute early!

Winston viewed up close, and standing tall,
in all it's glory, with the spectacular, 'grade two listed,'
Bennerley Viaduct, seen in the distance. There are
plans to restore the latticed ironwork viaduct
for walking and cycling (Note: this picture was taken in
the midday sun and gives all the appearance of mist)

Where have all the pits gone?

The smaller pits became uneconomical and were gradually filled in. The major ones, deep mines covering huge tracts of land have also been cleared away and the land restored to its former environmentally friendly condition. In many cases even better than our ancestors would remember. Wet scrubland and water meadows have been converted into lakes and parkland.

 A perfect example of this is nearby **Colliers Wood,** a nature reserve, free for all to enjoy. And in the valley where Moorgreen Colliery once echoed to the sound of miners' boots as legions of men reported for work, now there is silence.

This deep mine was the most important of the Barber Walker pits and Fionn Taylor writes of its strong productive seams in his website tribute to Ilkeston Mines Rescue and the memory of Philip Healey 1954 – 1971.

http://www.healeyhero.co.uk/rescue/pits/mooregreen

In 1930 over 150 men were seriously injured underground in the infamous Moorgreen mining accident, when the railway trucks they were travelling on ran out of control.

They and their relatives paid the heavy price of extracting coal from the bowels of the earth.

Not only has this land been reclaimed for a wide variety of leisure pursuits but events take place in the summer such as open air concerts and dog shows. In 2008 the site was awarded a green flag for excellent maintenance and community involvement.

'The Friends of Colliers Wood' hold monthly meetings with an active project agenda for the future. Many trees have been planted through the partnership with Greenwood Forests: Notts County Council and Broxtowe Borough Council.

The lake at Colliers Wood

The land that previously housed **Brinsley Colliery,** another nearby deep pit, has also been turned into a superb nature trail, with the headstocks salvaged, and left as a permanent reminder of its mining heritage.

D. H. Lawrence's father worked at this pit, including other relatives.

As with Colliers Wood, Broxtowe Borough Council, owners of both sites, have developed the land for community use.

'Friends of Brinsley Headstocks' produce a leaflet explaining their objectives are to protect these last remaining timber headstocks in Nottinghamshire and to develop the wildlife potential.
www.Brinsleyheadstocks.org

Brinsley pit ceased coal production in the early 1930's and after many years the headstocks were returned to their original site at Brinsley village.

An interesting feature near the Brinsley Headstocks car park is Vine Cottage, and Lawrence's Aunt Polly lived here. When I stopped by, taking my snapshots of this old abandoned, and boarded up cottage on a cold February day of 2016 it looked a sorry sight, but the ground around was covered in hundreds of sparkling white snowdrops, as if to say:

'We're sorry Aunt Polly, we know that you've gone
And your home has long lost its glow
But we are still here, to show that we care
And to add just an early spring show'

Aunt Polly's husband James was killed in a mining accident down Brinsley Pit in 1880 and Lawrence drew on his memories of Aunt Polly and his Uncle James in his short stories:

'Odour of Chrysanthemums,' and in 'The Widowing of Mrs Holroyd.' It is said the young David Herbert Lawrence loved this house and would spend many happy hours here in the orchard and gardens with his sister Ada.

There were plans afoot a few years to restore this cottage'

It was featured in an article written by Laura Rand in 2012 for the Eastwood and Kimberly Advertiser. I later had a conversation with Angela Smith who lived close by, and she explained a close friend Mr. Kinton was hoping to restore the building to its former glory and preserve it as an important museum for the benefit of visitors, schools and students of English literature. However plans must have fallen through, possibly through a lack of funding in these difficult times.

Brinsley village and colliery has known more than its fair share of tragedy over the years, and Stan Smith of Brinsley writes of this in his Brinsley books and 'Ztan Zmith' blogspot:

Harry Riley's footnote: Sad to relate that Stan Smith passed away 13th April
2016 and will be sadly missed by me and my sister–in-law Mavis Cordon, who contributed several articles for his publications, friends and relatives, and all those who remember him from his many books of the local areas. Including the famous 'Basford Bystander' magazine that has 'ex-pat' customers from all over the world buying on-line.

Basford Bystander

Basford & District Community Newspaper

Covering Old and New Basford, Aspley, Cinderhill, Hyson Green, Carrington, Radford, Broxtowe, Highbury Vale etc

February/March 2013   Every Other Month   35p

Sallis Athletic Football Team on Cinderhill Park in 1957

Contents

The Pot Man's Son - pt 2
Dennis & Barlock Typewriter Company
Tommy Morecroft, Albert & Mr Hyson
Dog Whipper & Peter's Pence
All's Well - Samuel Hall v Joseph Pearson
Berridge Road School 1940-1954
Bulwell Remembered - part 5

Issue 156

Plus regular feature:
Monthly Diary with meetings of clubs, societies, churches and local organisations.

Vine Cottage 2016

....

***Moorgreen Reservoir** was built in 1796 to supply water to Nottingham Canal. It is now a favourite venue for nature and literature lovers as they walk the Lawrence trails. The reservoir features in several of his novels and is well used by anglers*

Moorgreen Reservoir

Beauvale Lodge. Bridleway and entrance to Beauvale House Moorgreen, (built in 1873 for the 7th Earl Cowper)

Passing through the Beauvale Lodge gateway, the woodland walk along by the reservoir leads all the way towards the 17th century Annesley Hall and Park Estate. This fine old building has sadly fallen into ruinous decay since the Chaworth Musters family moved away to Felley Priory in the 1970's.

Lord Byron the poet was once romantically involved with Mary Anne Chaworth. She is said to be the lost love of his life.

Adjacent to the Hall is the ruined Annesley Old Church. This 'grade 2' listed building has been saved from further decay by a timely Lottery Heritage Grant and topped off to become safe for visitors and summer open air events.

In the graveyard are buried members of the Chaworth Musters family.

See http://www.ournottinghamshire.org.uk by Eastwood mining historian Dr. David Amos. (Project manager for the three-year Heritage Lottery Grant.)

Lawrence writes about Annesley Old Church in his novel 'The White Peacock'

and 'Byron' waxes lyrical about the Hall and Park in his poem 'The Dream.'

Colliers Wood and Brinsley Headstocks are both within a mile or so of Eastwood Town Centre and a little further afield is **Shipley Country Park.**

This elegant park has been created on the site of yet another large ex-coalfield and abuts to Heanor Town and Shipley Village.

The park covers 700 acres and boasts a Visitor Centre with shop. It is owned by Derbyshire county Council and was opened in 1976.

http://www.derbyshire.gov.uk

The Miller Mundy family owned Shipley Hall and mined this vast estate for two hundred years, until coal Mining Nationalisation in 1948. Coal production continued until the early 1960's but the manor house was demolished as being too badly effected by mining subsidence. Lodges and a water tower still remain and the park is a magnificent leisure facility for all to enjoy, with mature woodland walks and lakes to explore.

....

Felley Priory: Gardens: Nursery and Tea Room

Felley Priory Gardens are situated in North Nottinghamshire, hidden half a mile from the M1 motorway: (junction 27.)

This stunning, tranquil garden, where visitors will find many rare and unusual plants is one of Nottinghamshire's best kept secrets. The house and its 2.5 acre gardens are nestled in the most beautifully un-spoilt rolling countryside. The garden has been planted so that there are plants of interest all year round.

Felley Priory has a fully stocked nursery, from which visitors can purchase competitively priced plants which they have seen in the garden. There is also the **Farmhouse Tea Room,** which offers a delicious selection of light lunches, snacks and drinks.

About the house:

The priory of Felley was founded in 1156 on the site of a small hermitage dedicated to 'Our Lady.' It consisted of twelve canons following the Rule of Saint Augustine. They lived well organised lives, with a 'Stew Pond' for the Carp they ate on Fridays (which can be seen over the bottom garden wall) and a mile at the bottom of the hill.

Following the 'Dissolution' in 1535, not all of the Priory was completely destroyed. Parts were used elsewhere in the construction of the house and garden, for example, on the west side of the house between the Tudor Door and Chimney. The pillars at the entrance to the garden were originally part of the Priory Church and date from the late 12th. Century.

The brick side of the house, next to the old Jardonelle Pear Tree, dates from 1557, but it is thought that the Cloisters were within this area. The rest of the Priory was located towards the west end of the house. The garden now covers the site of the Priory Church. The high garden wall to the south west is believed to be part of the Priory boundary wall.

The central part of the house was constructed in the 16th and 17th Centuries. There is a particularly fine example of a Tudor Chimney on the west side of the house. The lion and unicorn on the west side of the house dates from this period.

The house was plundered during the Civil War and became an army garrison and a Royalist stronghold. The stone ends of the house were added about 1860 and the garden terraced in 1890. The pond in the garden may have been constructed then.

The Chaworth-Musters family became owners of the property in 1822, although they did not live there.

In 1973, Major Robert Chaworth-Musters moved to Felley, having sold Annesley Hall, the family home, which is just the other side of the M1 motorway. The Gardens were created thereafter by Major and Mrs. Chaworth-Musters.

The house is currently occupied by Major Chaworth-Musters' grandchildren: Sophia and Victoria, together with their father and step-mother.

The Chaworth Family:

12th Century-Patricius Chaworth arrived from France and settled in the Vale of Belvoir.

1440-George Chaworth married the heiress Alice Annesley who brought with her the estate of Annesley, where her family had lived for 300 years.

1628-George Chaworth was raised to the peerage by Charles 1st as Viscount Chaworth.

1765-William, Viscount Chaworth, was killed in a duel in London after an augument with his cousin and neighbour: Lord Byron (great uncle of the poet.)

1805-Mary Ann Chaworth, heiress of Annesley, married John Musters of Colwick Hall, near Nottingham, creating the name of Chaworth-Musters.

1831-While the Annual Goose Fair was taking place in Nottingham a messenger galloped in with the news that the Second Reform Bill had been thrown out of Parliament, and the already excited crowd had to be dispersed by the Militia.

The next day the crowd reformed, burned down Nottingham Castle and proceeded to sack Colwick Hall. Mrs. Chaworth Musters, with her daughter Sophia, soaking wet in the pouring rain, crouched all night in the shrubbery while the house was looted and set on fire. She died at Wiverton a few months later from the shock.

1832-Following these events the Chaworth-Musters family mainly lived at Annesley Hall.

1973-Major Robert Patricius Chaworth-Musters, who served in the Coldstream Guards, sold the Hall and moved to Felley Priory, which his family had owned since 1822.

1974-He married Maria Monkton, daughter of the 8th Viscount Galway of Serlby Hall in North Nottinghamshire and together they started creating the garden as it is today.

2010-Maria Chaworth-Musters dies and Major Chaworth- Musters' grandchildren: Sophia and Victoria, along with their father and step-mother move into Felley Priory.

The Garden:

The garden is comparatively new in relation to the house, which dates back to the 12th Century. An old photograph of the 1880's shows a sloping field and it is not until the 1890's that the ground was terraced.

The present layout dates from 1976. The priory is 600ft. above sea level and very exposed, so the first thing that Maria Chaworth-Musters, the creator of the garden, planted were the Yew Hedges as shelter for the herbaceous borders.

This is a garden for all seasons: **Spring** sees rare Snowdrops and Hellibores, followed by an orchard carpeted by Daffodils. The annual carpet of daffodils in the orchard, some of which are extremely rare, were recently the subject of a detailed article in The English Garden Magazine. The carpet of yellow, apricot, white and orange is a sight to behold during March and April. Colourful Tulips have recently been added to the garden. Other plants grown at this time of the year include a wonderful collection of Magnolias, Snake's Head Fritillery, which underplants the trees in the specimen shrubbery area, Hellibores, and finally a stunning collection of both Herbaceous and Tree Peonies, some of which are very old.

Note: a stunning woodland carpet of Bluebells can also be found at Felley Priory in the Spring.

Summer:

Summer Highlights include scented roses and colourful herbaceous borders, creating a spectacular display. The walled rose garden is filled with old- fashioned roses - Gallicias, Bourbons, Moss Roses, Damasks, Albas and Chinensis. Under the old Elizabethan wall are many Agapanthus and some tender shrubs. The borders around the walls have a mixture of trees and shrubs underplanted by Geraniums Hostas, Digitalis and Meconopsis, amongst others.

In the centre of the garden, the pergolas are covered with roses, vines, clematis and lonicera, and are surrounded by a knot garden made up of architectural box and yew topiary birds. This area was one of the first parts of the garden to be established and was designed to reflect the age and brickwork of the Priory itself.

Autumn:

As the Summer closes there is still plenty to see at Felley Priory. An extensive collection of Hydrangeas provide wonderful Autumn colour throughout the garden, including some which are very rare and therefore are not often seen. Many of the trees have beautiful Autumnal shades of red and orange to enjoy, along with pale mauve and white Colchicums.

Winter:

The Topiary is the original framework from which the garden was established and in Winter it is still an outstanding feature. Even when snow-covered, the garden's topiary is magnificent, with the bushes shaped into Swans, Castles, and Peacocks.

The start of the year heralds the arrival of 60 varieties of snowdrops. The collection is made up of the usual white snowdrops, as well as some rarer yellow types, including Wendy's Gold, Sandersii Group Ray Cobb, Spindleson Surprise and primrose Warburg, to name but a few.

Opening Times:

The Garden, Nursery and Tea Rooms are open: Tuesday to Friday-year round, 9am to 4pm. The first and third Sunday of each month, from 1st February until 4th October, 10am until 4pm.
Coaches welcome by appointment.

(Please Note: Felley Priory is a private house, and not open to the public.)

Entrance Pricing:
March to October: £5:00 Adult. £4:50 OAP 2017.
October to March: £4:50 per person 2017.

Children under 16 Free.

RHS members free admission Tuesdays and Wednesdays only.

Venue Accessibility:

Both the Garden and the Tea Rooms are accessible to those in wheelchairs, with disabled toilets in addition.

Cars can park down to the Nursery for those who do not wish to walk from the car park.

(No dogs or picnics are allowed on site.)

The Tea Rooms:
The Farmhouse Tea Room opened in 2011. With both indoor and outdoor seating in what was the old Farmhouse, the Tea Room offers a delicious selection of homemade cakes, scones, light lunches and beverages.
The Tea Room can be hired as a venue for private events.

The Nursery:
Many of the plants on display in the garden are available to buy in the Nursery. Which stocks rare and unusual plants as well as cottage garden favourites.

The knowledgeable team of staff are always in the Nursery to offer advice on where to plant, and how to look after your purchases.

Felley Priory Contact:

Michelle Upchurch

Felley Priory Gardens

Underwood

Nottingham

NG16 5FJ

T: 01773 801230

Website: http://www.felleypriory.co.uk

Email: info@felleypriory.co.uk

Felley Priory

41

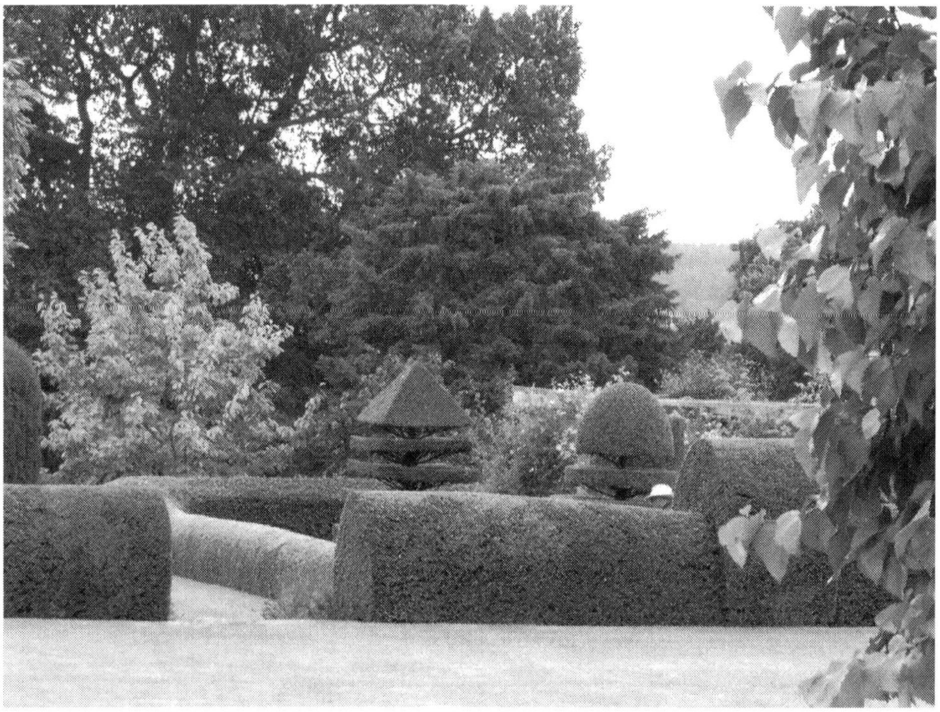

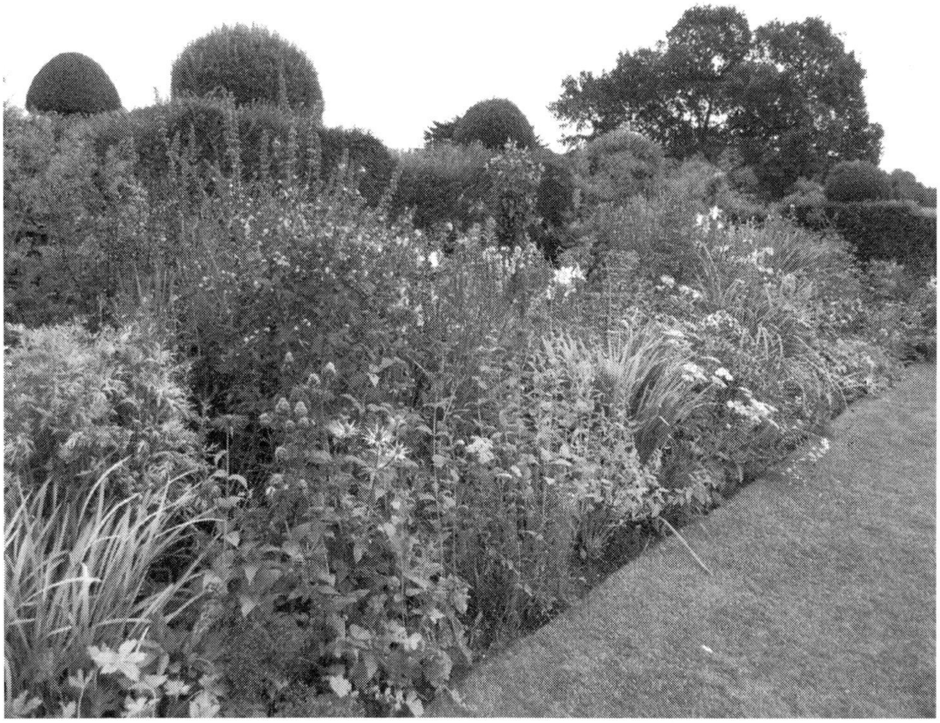

Views photographed by Harry Riley at Felley Priory, August 2016

....

Eastwood Hall

The Hall was built in 1810 by the Walker family who were instrumental in building up one of Britains major coal mining companies. The house is now a grade 2 listed building, to the west of Eastwood town and is set in 26 acres of parklands.

Later taken over by the National Coal Board, the Hall became their regional headquarters, and during the 1980's miners strike it was the operational headquarters of British Coal.

In the 1990's the hall continued to operate during the gradual privatization of the mines in 1994 and was used as a base whilst other assets, mainly land and property were sold off.

In 1996 the house was put on the market by British Coal and purchased in 1997 by North Nottingham developer: Strawson Holdings, who also bought several other British Coal properties.

The house was sold to Hayley Conference Centres and plans for development were submitted in March 1999.
It was opened in May 2000 and was later bought out by Principal Hotels in May
2007.
Contact: **www.principal-hayley.com**

(information above is courtesy of their fact sheet.)

Eastwood Hall

....

Chapter 2: Purposeful Lives

Ellie Lodziak Leatherland

When I moved to Eastwood with my young family 40 years ago, I wanted to become involved in the community that had made me so welcome. For a few years I was a foster mum and had several part-time jobs. I did notice signs of high unemployment affecting young people in our town so when I saw an advertisement in the local paper for a part-time youth worker with EYUP (Eastwood Young Unemployed Project) I applied and got the job.

This was the start of a long career in community involvement, including the development of Eastwood People's Initiative (EPI.)
This project aspired to meet the needs of local people by providing services that they themselves had identified, such as Welfare Rights and unemployment advice, food parcels, homelessness support and a place of refuge.

I was also persuaded to venture into politics and served for six years on Eastwood Town Council and eight years as a Nottinghamshire County Councillor. Although I had never had ambitions in this direction, I felt very privileged to have the opportunity to represent people and have a voice on issues that affected them. For example, young people desperately wanted a new Youth Centre and with their help I worked hard with officers at County Hall to secure the funding for this wonderful building.

Although I officially retired seven years ago and am now a grandma and great-grandma I will always have a passion for my community so I am still involved with EPI, celebrating 34 years with the charity this year.
I have made some lovely friends along the way, met some extraordinary people and hopefully made some small contribution to the community I call home.
Ellie Lodziak Leatherland

....

'The White Peacock Coffee House' 33 Scargill Walk Eastwood Notts. and 'St. John Ambulance Charity Day.'

The North Notts Fellowship St. John Ambulance-a group of retired members of the St. John Ambulance were invited to organize a Fund-Raising event for The St. John Eye Hospital in Jerusalem who are the only charitable providers of eye-care, and the leading providers for the fight against preventable blindness in Jerusalem, Gaza and The West Bank.

The rates of blindness in the Holy Land are ten times higher than in the west, 80% of blindness being preventable.

The hospital resources go as far as taking their Mobile Units into area where people can be treated.

Walk-in cases at the hospital are helped and never refused treatment.

At the St. John Hospital over a three-year period approximately 40,000 individuals have been screened for various eye problems and disease. Plus, since November 2012, over 26,000 patients have been treated with eye conditions including many with Cataracts.

With help from 'Fundraising' from our Groups in England and elsewhere we are ensuring the work of this wonderful hospital can carry on into the future.

Pauline Dowsing, along with Pat Bailey and Kate Lishman would like to express their thanks to Pauline's son-in-law and daughter, Paul and Julie Betts and their daughter Sophie, the owners of the White Peacock Coffee House, for allowing them to have the use of their premises for the day. Thank you also to their customers for their support and to the local community for their support in helping to raise £73:50 for our Hospital in Jerusalem. Once Again, Many Thanks!
(St. John Ambulance is a company limited by Guarantee)

Note: The White Peacock Coffee House is open 9am to 2pm
T: 07837 306234

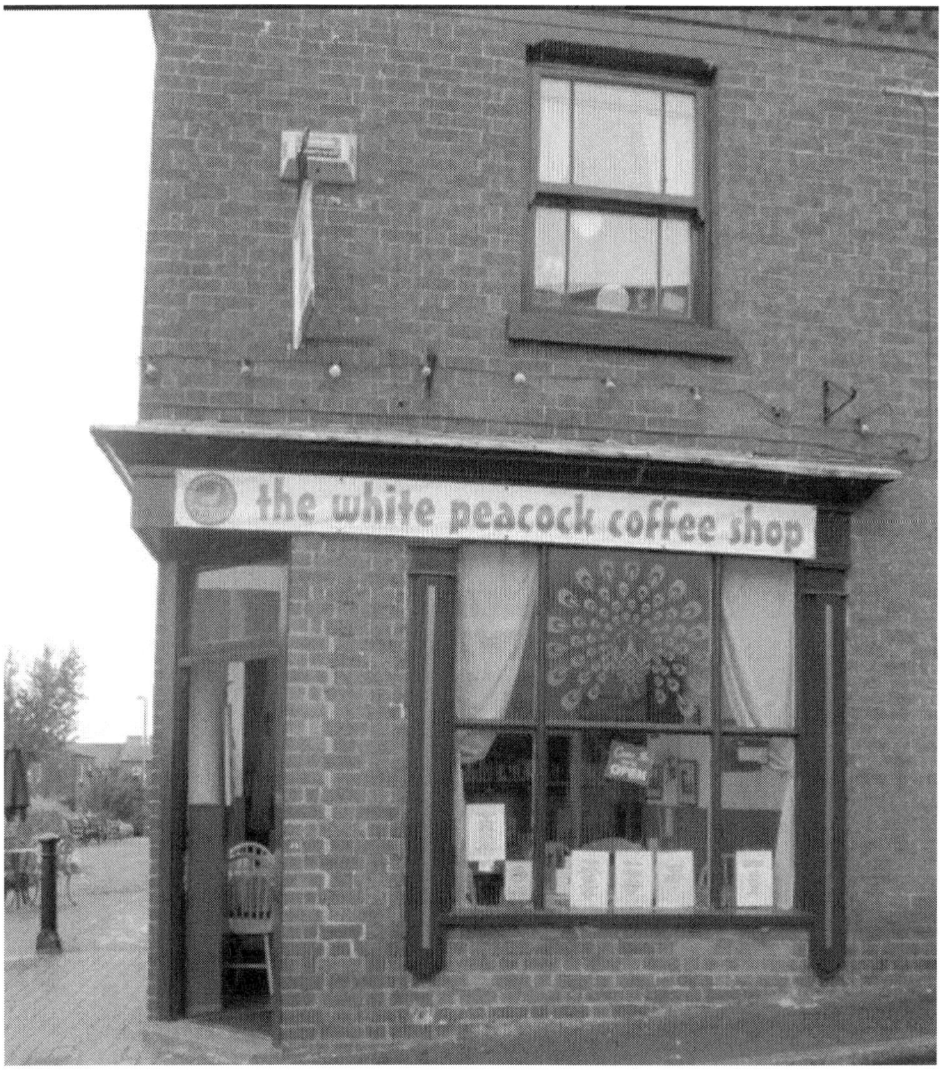
the white peacock coffee shop
OPEN

White Peacock Eastwood: Serving Delicious food!
See them on facebook-for good reviews from satisfied customers,
tourists and locals.

....

A Team with a Dream:

By the early 1960's over 4000 tons of pit waste had been unceremoniously dumped in the Langley Mill Canals Basin by the closing of Moorgreen Colliery. It did not concern British Coal unduly because the canal system was already neglected and derelict anyway, and so who cared?

Some people were concerned to save and salvage the remaining waterways. Folk who treasured the memory of bygone days and appreciated the long lost beauty of horses trotting along a canal bank and perhaps towing a slow narrowboat. A time when folk would stop to chat or listen to the sound of nature, but surely, it was far too late to restore a system of travel that had succumbed to the passage and progress of the industrial revolution.

In any case British Waterways themselves had accepted defeat.

Derby, Cromford and Nottingham Canals had gone, and only the Eerewash Canal remained against all the odds. Fortunately it had not been snatched by the railways.

But the facts remained, who could perform a miracle? Who had the strength and the courage and the ability and the fortitude and the backing, and most of all the will and wherewithal to take on, and to tackle such an enormous task that would and could run on for years. Surely it had to be celebrity superstars who could wave their magic wands and orchestrate such a fantastically wonderful transformation.

However we are not writing about a team of super-fit young athletes in their prime, with the backing of wealthy sponsors and their bottomless pockets, to take on the doubters and prevaricators and *jobsworths* who would stand in their way, with their reasoned arguments and endless red tape. They were there in abundance. Make no mistake!

It was literally to be 'down to earth' Nottinghamshire and Derbyshire folk, who refused to take no for an answer. The sort of hands-on-people, capable of superhuman tasks: people who have always been the backbone of the Nation. It would be a dirty, dangerous job to dig out those many tons of rubble and to replace the banks and lock gates, and eventually to re-water. There would be bridges to reconstruct, favours to ask, and it would all cost time and money.

And so the team was formed and given a name: The ECP&DA which stands for: the Erewash Canal Preservation and Development Association. They were not in it for the money, but were volunteers, proud to make a difference.

The proof of what they achieved is now clear for all to see and to wonder at. A magnificent sight to behold! With a restored Erewash Canal and Langley Mill Basin, navigable all the way to the river Trent at Trent Lock. A swing-bridge that really works, and is the only one still functioning for many miles around: the fully restored and refurbished Nottingham Toll Office and a Victorian pumping station, all on site.

To the visitor or casual observer it seems as though it may have always been thus, it all looks so natural: the long boats moored up, and the canal locks and the well-kept towpaths, and the clean water filled with Carp and Roach and all manner of freshwater fish, and the Water Voles and Frogs and Dragon Flies and the Mallards and Coots and Waterhens: the hedgerows teeming with birdlife, Kingfishers and Yellow Hammers and Reed Buntings, Robins and Blue Tits etc.

If anyone asks of the true nature of conservation in Notts and Derbyshire, you need point no further than this, and the unstinting charitable work of the ECP&DA charity and its volunteers.

During our visit (Brian and I) we met several volunteers, John Baylis, Paul, and Howard, all extremely helpful, and it was Paul who took time out from his volunteer duties to show us around the fully restored Victorian Pumping Station, the renovated Nottingham Toll Office and the planned restoration of a section of the Cromford Canal, which has been put on hold, but which is still a feasible proposition for the future.

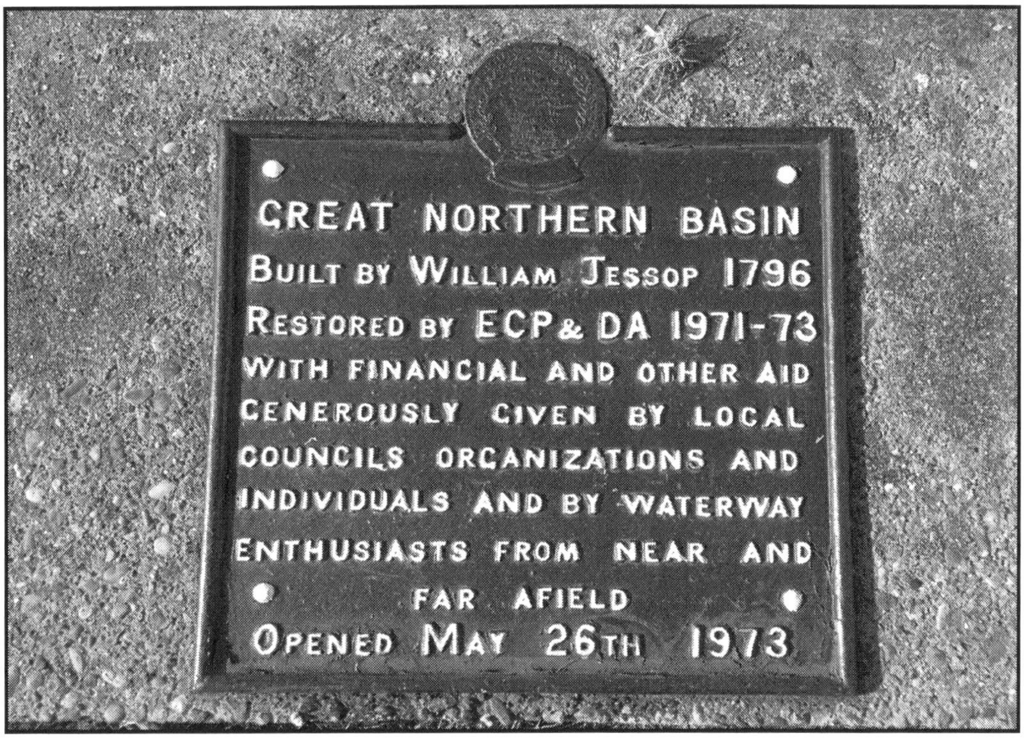
GREAT NORTHERN BASIN
BUILT BY WILLIAM JESSOP 1796
RESTORED BY ECP& DA 1971-73
WITH FINANCIAL AND OTHER AID
GENEROUSLY GIVEN BY LOCAL
COUNCILS ORGANIZATIONS AND
INDIVIDUALS AND BY WATERWAY
ENTHUSIASTS FROM NEAR AND
FAR AFIELD
OPENED MAY 26TH 1973

The fully restored Nottingham Toll House

The Swing Bridge

Inside the Pump House

John Baylis B.E.M. Chair of Cromford Canal Friends

Nottingham Canal Toll Office

Left to Right: John Baylis B.E.M : Prince Michael of Kent: Sir Alfred McAlpine, President of TT. At the Trinity House Presentation, alluded to above.

Chapter 3: A Country Park

Still keeping with the pits and coal-mining theme, transporting coal to Leicestershire and the West Midlands was not an easy task and this is why the canal waterways were so vital, particularly before the railways.

There were so many pits springing up in and around North Notts and Derbyshire that funds were found by the coal-masters to dig out these narrow waterways and link them up. Before long we had the Erewash Canal: the Cromford, and the Nottingham Canal. A short link had to be cut to join the deep Shipley Colliery, and so towards the end of the 1790's, the four and a half mile long Nutbrook Canal was created from Shipley Wharf to the Erewash Canal.

It had 13 locks and although much of it has now been split into lagoons, just like the Nottingham Canal, we still have the Nutbrook Trail for walkers to enjoy, going all the way to Long Eaton.

For three centuries the Miller Mundy's owned the Shipley estate that is now Shipley Country Park, run by Derbyshire County Council.

The wealthy Miller Mundy family built a huge stone mansion with the ground floor containing 20 rooms. They employed many servants on this 700 acre estate and entertained royalty.

At various times the family would include an admiral and a Lord Lieutenant of the County. This hall was built in the middle of the estate, being the jewel in the crown, of which Alfred Miller Mundy was sole owner and lord of the manor.

The family were to become Coalmasters.

Over the years several deep pit shafts have been sunk on and around this land.

It was coal that preserved and extended their wealth and influence, and it was coal that eventually caused the handsome Hall to subside and to be demolished.

The Nottingham and Derby Lodges and Home Farm are private within the park, as is the Water Tower and several other buildings.

The Suffragette Wall still stands, and Derbyshire County Council has generously provided attractive information boards at strategic points for interested visitors to study.

The Miller Mundy potted history and heraldic coats of Arms can be seen at the House footings with a plan of the house and gardens, just as they would have looked.

Many hundreds of trees have been planted and events continue throughout the season, including **Erewash and Amber Valley 'Footsteps Festival'** annually during September. Of which both Brian Fretwell and I have participated, leading walks. **http://www.autumnfootprints.co.uk**,

Harry Riley's note:

All walks free of charge, although on some walks, car parks may carry a parking charge

All that is left of Shipley Colliery, viewed from The Parkland across Shipley Lake in 2016

Today Shipley Country Park has plenty to offer visitors, and with coffee shops and a Visitor Centre there are many diverse outdoor activities to pursue.

....

Chapter 4: Community Stalwarts

Albert Wardle was born on 25th April 1929. He was the second son of Annie and John Wardle and lived on Raglan St. and then Lyncroft, Eastwood. He suffered from Diptheria as a youngster, and was educated at Greasley Beauvale School and then went on to Eastwood County Secondary School, where he became Head Boy.

His hobby at that time was breeding and keeping Budgies and showing them.

Always keen on sport, he played both cricket and football for local teams. His love of music was to be a constant thread throughout his life, playing piano, and church organ at Eastwood Church as a teenager.

Albert's first job was in the Barber Walker office and in 1947 aged 18 he joined the Grenadier Guards. During his time in the Grenadiers' he visited Buckingham Palace on a number of occasions including the presentation of new Colours, Queens Company, First Battalion, based at RHQ.

His musical talent was to stand him in good stead, as he was to play the piano in the Grenadier Dance Band in London.

However he never forgot his roots and whilst home on weekend leave he would play the organ at Eastwood Church.

Albert retired from the Grenadier Guards as a Sergeant in 1954 with an exemplary Military Record.

In the same year he married Margaret and they lived at Lyncroft before moving to Nottingham Road Giltbrook and then to Heather Close where they had 3 children: Angela: Kathryn and Richard.

After his army career Albert was employed at Moorgreen Colliery in the Time office and then he went into the Prison Service, where he stayed for 22 years.

Outside of work he continued to enjoy sport: club football: cricket for Eastwood St. Mary's and umpiring for Greasley Church.

The Eastwood Branch of the British Legion benefitted from a decade where he was their chairman: 205-2015, and he served on the Midlands Area Co-Operative Board and acting Treasurer of Eastwood Probus.

Being a community-minded music lover, Albert was organist and choirmaster at Greasley Church for 41 years and wrote his own music to 'The Lord's Prayer,' which incidentally was played at his funeral. Sadly he died 22nd December 2015

A man of many talents, Albert leaves his widow Margaret, 3 children and 4 grandchildren.

Albert Wardle : 25th April 1929-22nd Dec.2015

....

Don Rowley

Our next community stalwart is **Don Rowley,** and he was born at 'The Breach' Eastwood 1932.

Attending Beauvale Boys School from 5-11 he then went on to Walker Street, County Secondary School (A classes.)

When called up for National Service he served in the Royal Artillery as a Radar Operator at Owestry, moving on to Wales, Norfolk and Cornwall. At two of these postings he was Captain of the football team, winning several medals, (telling people he was a decorated army Captain!)

Then in 1959 Don joined Birnam Products and enjoyed 39 happy years, becoming Forman, Quality Assessor, Stand-in Personnel Manager and Works Pension Trustee. He continued his sporting activities, becoming President of the 'works football 1' team.

In 1991 a very dear friend: Councillor Hazel Braithwaite coaxed him into standing as a Labour Party Candidate for Eastwood Town Council and he was elected in 1995.

Following on from this success Don became Mayor of Eastwood and a Broxtowe Borough Councillor (twice declining the Mayorship.)

By 2004 he became Leader of Eastwood Town Council. During his tenure, Eastwood became the first minor authority in Nottinghamshire to achieve 'Quality Council Accreditation.'

Outside of politics Don served as President of Eastwood Collieries Male Voice Choir for 19 years: twice President of Eastwood and District Probus Club: President of Eastwood Age Concern: Vice President of Heanor Hospital League of Friends: Vice Chair of Eastwood C.A.B: Governor of Eastwood Comprehensive School, and Lyncroft Junior School.

Whilst Mayor of Eastwood in 2002 he initiated the Mayor's Award Scheme and was a prime mover in twinning Eastwood Town with Szolnok Hungary.

The first visit to Szolnok being in 2004.

Don is still a collector for Cancer Research and and the Royal British Legion.

Footnote: Birnam Products was a major Eastwood Employer and Don was the first of their 700 Employees to be invited to join the Directors as a Company Pensions Trustee.

Don and His wife Marjorie at award ceremony with the members of the Eastwood Collieries Male Voice Choir.

Note: A fascinating history of the renowned Eastwood Collieries Male Voice Choir 1995: entitled 'Music all Powerful' by Michael Pope (thirty five years a Choir member) He dedicates this history to the late Granville Mee, and other old friends who are now 'Singing in God's Choir in the Sky'

MUSIC ALL POWERFUL

EASTWOOD COLLIERIES'
MALE VOICE CHOIR
1920 - 1995

Don's own copy of this 75th anniversary gem

Don and his wife Marjorie

Don Rowley very kindly lent our researcher: Brian Fretwell, a copy of Eastwood Training Corps and Lads Club Jubilee 1900 -1950 Souvenir Brochure. This was originally priced at one shilling and is now a priceless mine of information, of the how: the where: the why: and the who: of this very important young boys organization.

Eastwood Training Corps and Lads' Club

1900   1950

NON SIBI

Jubilee Souvenir
BROCHURE

PRICE ONE SHILLING

....

Eastwood's new (£2 million pound) Youth Centre, Managed by Andy Allsopp:

Harry Riley's note:

I first met Andy during **'World Book Night,'** a few years ago.

Together with Sarah Taylor and a further teacher from Eastwood Comprehensive School, we had several dozen brand new books to give away, on behalf of **The Reading Agency's World Book Night.**

The evening we had arranged was to be in two parts. The main event was a couple of hours entertainment At **Eastwood's Dun-Lite Coffee House,** with 'Book Readings' by local authors, and the highlight being a concert by the **Community Choir.** During this event we were giving away books to people who would not normally read them.

After this event I crossed Eastwood Town Centre, along with Councillor Keith Longdon, and visited the new Youth Centre. We met with Andy (Centre Manager) by appointment, and presented some of his young members with books on behalf of **World Book Night,** and our own fledgling org: Eastwood

Booktown Development Group.

Recently we asked Andy to contribute a few words for this vol. Two, and here, written in his own words, is his own story:

'My name is Andy Allsopp and I am a Youth worker for Notts County Council and have worked in Eastwood for 15 years now.

I started in the youth club based on the Eastwood Comprehensive School site. However I was not there too long as our lease came to an end and the school wanted the building to create a new reception and extend their arts and drama block. We were then essentially homeless for many years, not that this was a real problem as we used to meet groups of young people on the parks and streets and engage them in positive activities and offer information advice and support.

We would often get the minibus and go on trips and visits. Also, for many years we had a Mobile-Youth-Bus that used to park on Coronation Park: Jubilee Park: and Iceland Car Park every week, offering arts and sports activities as well as a warm drink in the winter months.

This vehicle was really popular and we would often be quite a squeeze, but it was cosy and young people could rely on it being there for them. I do miss those days on the streets and parks but I always knew that the youth of Eastwood deserved something better, and that is why I made it my goal to help raise funds and work alongside young people to design a youth centre that was big and special, and to be an asset to the town I had come to think of as a second home. The search for a place to locate the youth centre was a long and frustrating journey, and don't get me started on the politics.

However we had a very committed steering group of young people that stayed with it and eventually saw their hard work and time come to fruition. On Friday the ninth of September 2011 we had the official opening of the 2 million pound, Young People's Centre with Councillor Keith Walker formally opening the building, in the presence of Lord-Lieutenant of Nottinghamshire, Sir Andrew Buchanan.

The centre was a hit from the start and we were and still are to this day really busy both day and night. We continue to have happy, challenging, difficult, and dare I say hectic times at the centre, but one thing is for sure: the town needed this place and that has been reflected in crime and anti-social behaviour figures and also told to me by former service users that come back to see us when they are older, appreciative and full of nostalgia.'

Andy Allsopp outside the Youth Centre

77

Eastwood Town Mayor: Councillor Keith Longdon with Youth Centre members.

....

Our 'Stalwarts' theme continues with **Horace Webster: 1908-1969.**

Horace was born in Sutton in Ashfield. On the completion of his school education he became articled to E.S.B. Hopkin at Mansfield, the firm of solicitors providing legal support to Eastwood Urban District Council. Horace was soon appointed the Council's first directly employed Clerk, later becoming Clerk and Chief Financial Officer to Eastwood Urban District Council, remaining in that post until his death.

In 1935 Horace and his wife Madge moved to Eastwood where their two daughters: Pamela and Eileen were born.

Living in the town, Horace walked from his home to his office four times each day. He knew the business and trades people, the shopkeepers, the shoppers, and the townspeople. He noticed the cleanliness and condition of the town daily and ensured that any deficiencies were quickly rectified.

With the outset of the Second World War he initiated 'Holidays at Home' and came to know all the volunteers who helped to run the scheme. At this time he realised there was a need for facilities for girls uniformed groups (Guides, Brownies, St. John Cadets, Girl Clubs) to meet. The Lads' Club at the corner of Church St. provided well for the boys.

After losing a tenancy arrangement of the old school behind the parish church, there was a more urgent need to find a permanent home for the girls. A committee was formed to pursue this and Horace was appointed as its honorary organizing secretary. Leaders of the girl's groups and other interested people of the town began fund raising and looking for a suitable site on which to build.

Garden parties, Christmas fairs, concerts and social events all formed part of the funding effort under Horace's guidance and encouragement. The Rotary Club: The Inner Wheel Club and The Trades Guild were generous supporters and also worked with Horace to seek external funding for the ambitious scheme.

The then Ministry of Education was particularly unhelpful towards the venture. It seemed to have no vision for a scheme that would be the first of its kind in the country, offering a facility solely for use by girls' groups. In spite of many
disappointments the committee, with Horace at its helm persevered and the Eastwood Girls' Centre: The Dora Phillips Hall on Wood Street was erected. It was built by Vic Hallam to the highest standards of quality and workmanship and opened in September 1962.

Horace continued as voluntary secretary, leading the committee of supporters and management until he died in 1989.

Dora Phillips Hall Centre for Girls

The Eastwood Girls' Centre

In 1946 a committee for the Eastwood Centre for Women and Girls was formed. Its purpose was to respond to a need to provide and maintain accommodation for Women's and Girls' organisations in the town.

The original premises in Church Walk were used until 1951 when temporary accommodation at Church Street Community Centre became available.

It became clear that a permanent building was required and eventually this site in Wood Street was purchased in 1958.

Meanwhile the Girls' Centre Committee had been raising funds and together with special donations and gifts of materials this building was erected in 1962.

A Management Committee, with the approval of the Charities Commission, is responsible for the Centre which is provided primarily as a meeting place for girls' youth organisations and associated bodies in Eastwood. When not required by these groups the Centre is available for hire.

At the time of the opening on 15 September 1962, the Centre was unique in its objectives being the only youth centre known in Great Britain to be provided solely for girls' youth organisations.

50 years later the work continues. Hundreds of girls have benefited form using these excellent facilities and the Centre is currently home to
- 1st Eastwood Rainbow Guides
- 2nd Eastwood Rainbow Guides
- 1st Eastwood Brownie Guides
- 1st Eastwood Guides
- Eastwood District Ranger Guides
- St. John Ambulance Cadets

Associated bodies include
- Eastwood Arts Group
- Keep Fit
- W.I.
- Weightwatchers
- Co-operative Dance Group
- Children's Art Group

Why Dora Phillips Hall?

Mrs Dora Phillips who lived at the now demolished Eastwood Grange was one of the benefactors to the Centre

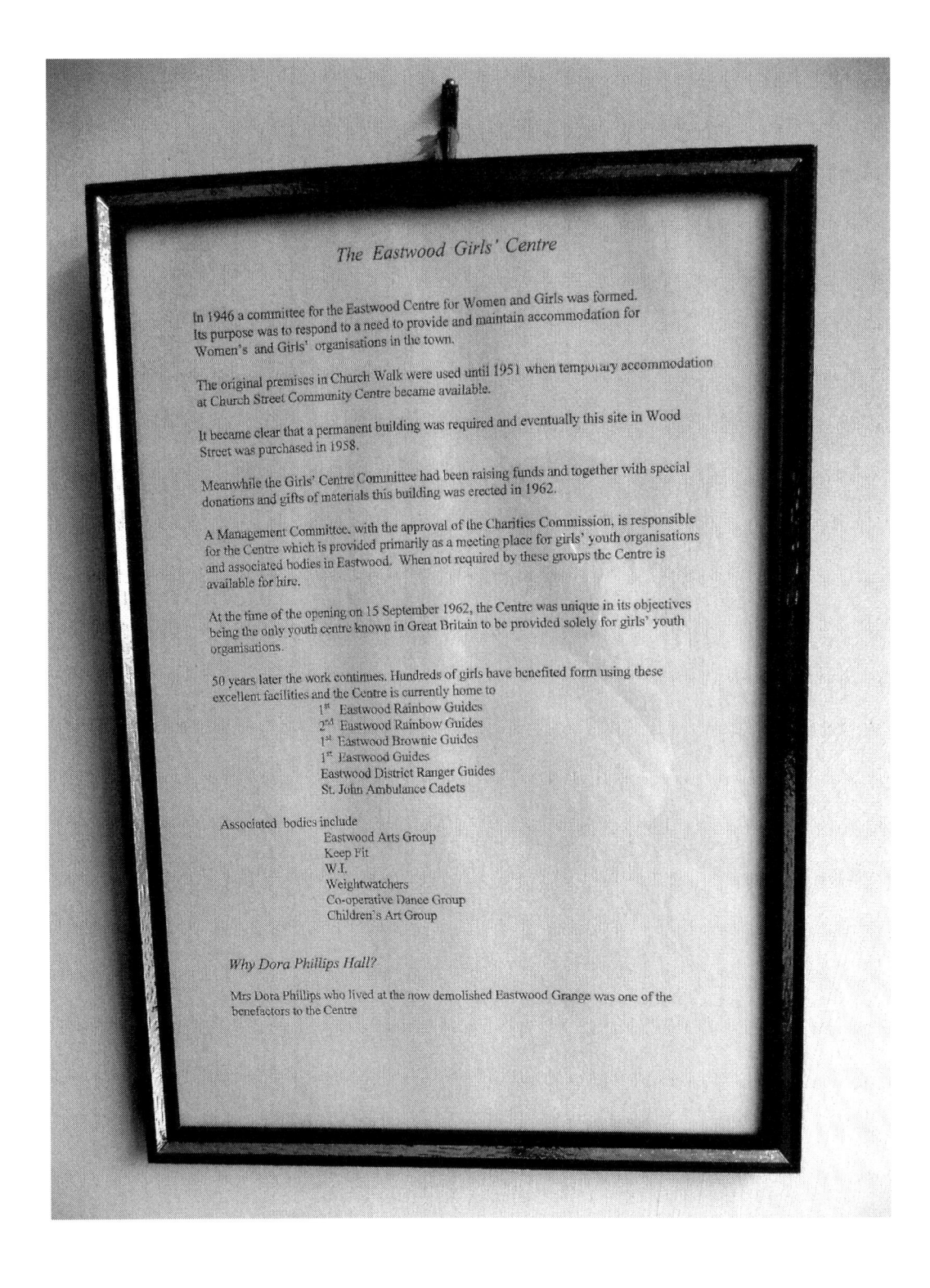

Horace Webster

TO THE AFFECTIONATE MEMORY
OF
HORACE WEBSTER
SECRETARY 1946 – 1969

IN APPRECIATION OF HIS LOYAL
SERVICE TOWARDS THE BUILDING
OF THIS
CENTRE FOR GIRLS

Jubilee Certificate

The St JOHN AMBULANCE BRIGADE

The Commissioner-in-Chief records his appreciation of

The Moorgreen Nursing Division

which has cared for the sick and suffering for a continuous period of **50** years thereby Maintaining the High Tradition of The Most Venerable Order of St. John

6th. June 1990   Commissioner-in-Chief

Pro Fide, Pro Utilitate Hominum

This is to Certify that 1st Eastwood COMPANY OF THE Girl Guides is duly registered at Headquarters.

Robert Baden-Powell
Founder.

Date 20th April 1927

Chapter 5: Health and Beauty

Eunice Taylor shares her memories of the shop she opened in Eastwood approx. 30 years ago:

'Since my name was Eunice Taylor, we called the shop; Taylor's Fashion Accessories. I had a fifteen-year lease on it, thinking it would be a good investment for my pension. I was 53 years old and already had a shop of the same name in Heanor. It was a very busy shop, especially a 'favourite' with the ladies, although men could buy good presents for their partners.

We sold everything you could imagine including jewellery: tights etc: bags: purses: scarves: hats: even umbrellas' many called it 'Alladin's Cave!'

Very much enjoyed was November lighting up night, when the town was absolutely full of visitors. Quite a few shops stayed open then and we all did fancy dress at our shop. Business was brisk and all customers received a glass of wine.

Eventually we did ear-piercing and later nose-piercing (very popular.)

After several years came harder times and quite a few shops around us closed. Boots, who were next door, moved further down into town.

Next door on the right, Fords went bankrupt and several more closed, including Machin and Hartwell across the road.

We managed to hang on until the lease finished, but we struggled with vandalism, windows broken and thieving. It was a shop people enjoyed, not only for the choice of goods, but also for the friendliness of staff.

To this day I meet women who say they wish it were still there. Trouble is things change, and not always for the better.'

Eunice Taylor and her shop colleagues

The Eastwood Dental Centre

The dental surgery in Eastwood was started by David O'Sullivan on Nottingham Road, above what used to be Sallinger's the opticians. He then bought 130 Nottingham Road, which had been a coal yard and extensively altered the building to give three surgeries on the first floor and a reception and waiting room on the ground floor, where Mr. O'Sullivan's mother lived.

David started to have kidney problems, so in 1971 he sold the practice to Alistair Shaw and Eric Reid, two young graduates from Dundee. Alastair and Eric installed new equipment and offered general anaesthetics with intravenous sedation, including Valium. Eric unfortunately contracted testicular cancer and died in 1974, leaving a young wife and daughter. He and Alastair had purchased another dental practice on Mansfield Road in Sherwood, so they were joined by Eric Seaman and David Hamilton. Michael Wojtowicz joined and became a partner in 1974 until 1995.

The practice continued to grow and a ground floor extension allowed another surgery manned by Trevor Archer. James Peachey, Ken Shaw and Bob Russell succeeded Eric Seaman and david Hamilton and later Bob Lewthwaite. In 1980 another extension was built above the entrance to the car park, allowing another four surgeries to be accommodated with Leo Jurkiw and John Foster taking those rooms over. Two of the original staff from 1971: Andrea Bikow and Pamela Durrance remained for many years.

August 2016:
The practice has continued to grow with many projects undertaken to expand the NHS dental service available to Eastwood and the surrounding areas.

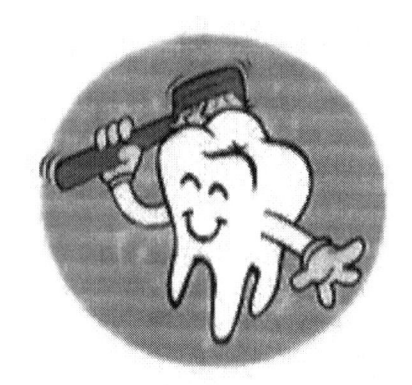

Chapter 6: Friend and Mentor of D. H. Lawrence

There was a time when the mention of William Edward Hopkin was well known around Eastwood and district for a variety of reasons. There was the family shoe shop in town started by his father. Then there were the open-house-forums where people of all political and religious persuasions would meet on a regular basis to air their views on anything under the sun. And then again there were the regular features in the Eastwood and Kimberley Advertiser called Rambling Notes emanating from the pen of William Hopkin, known to his friends as Willie. As if that were not all, this man of many talents was a magistrate, a County Councillor and had been a Mayor.

Eastwood Library has a wall plaque dedicated to William Hopkin and a collection of his books for reference only: (kept under lock and key, but clearly visible behind the glass case.

Harry Riley's note:

Tracy, the Library Manager, very kindly allowed me to photograph The W. E. Hopkin plaque and collection of books and in order to find out more about the man who'd been a close friend of D.H. Lawrence, I browsed the Internet and came up with a pleasantly 'surprising article' published by:

http://www.pennilesspress.co.uk./prose/W.E.Hopkin.htm

It is entitled : Eastwood and W. E. Hopkin (Willie) *Plus, Leslie Williamson (With a dash of D. H. Lawrence.)*

Publisher John Lucas very kindly allowed me to include details of this Leslie Williamson essay about the life and times of Willie Hopkin and his association with author D.H. Lawrence.

I say this is surprising because for several years I have been a member of Eastwood Writers Group of which the late Leslie Williamson was a previous Chair and Life President.

I never had the chance to meet Leslie as he died before I joined the group, but I have read a couple of his books: **'Jobey'** and **'Bread for All'**, both of which I really enjoyed. So with this article/essay from John Lucas we not only learn more about W. E. Hopkin but also about D.H.Lawrence, and another, more modern and very accomplished writer: Les Williamson. (Three birds with one stone, so to speak.)

W. E. Hopkin (portrait and inscription plate featured in Eastwood Library)

W. E. Hopkin Book Collection (containing editions of D. H. L. Books and articles.) in Eastwood Library

Caricature of Willie Hopkin

Bust of D. H. Lawrence in Eastwood Library
(1885-1930)

Large blow-up photograph of D. H. Lawrence and his German partner: Frieda in Eastwood Library

Harry Riley's note:

The D. H. Lawrence Society of Eastwood: dhlawrencesociety.com

has a thriving membership with a full programme of Events for 2016-17. Details can also be found on facebook and twitter and there is a world wide following of loyal fans.

Personally, nailing my colours to the mast, I have always been intrigued to discover how D.H. L. fares in the literary debate between that other great author (and my own personal favourite) Thomas Hardy. I have visited both their homes, each hailing from very modest parentage. I particularly enjoy D.H.L.'s short stories and his Etruscan Places –Italian essays.

However I have never tired of reading and re-reading T. H's novel: The Mayor of Casterbridge, and believe I've known several 'Michael Henchard's' in my life: successful businessmen, generous to a fault, who would willingly give you their last penny, but who could be the bitterest of enemies if once crossed. To my mind, Lawrence's T. Hardy critique, says more about himself and his own work than it does about Hardy and I found it very disappointing. Michael Henchard the Mayor of Casterbridge is as relevant to modern society as he ever was, whereas many of D.H.L's ancient fictional characters are really dead and buried. I'm sure there are many who will not agree, but that is just my own humble opinion.

For those wishing to join the D.H. Lawrence society or for more information : **email: dhlawrencesociety@gmail.com Chairman: Malcolm Gray: President: Professor John Worthen**

....

Eastwood and W. E. Hopkin (Willie)
(With a dash of D.H.Lawrence)
By Leslie Williamson

I write from the wilds of deepest Nottinghamshire where the merry men disported themselves in a land that is always summer and the sun shines every day-according to Hollywood. There, lived a grand old man who was well known and very much liked-not always the same thing.

William Edward Hopkin rather lived in the shadow of D.H. Lawrence, he died in 1951, but I knew him quite well (I suddenly feel quite old). I was a cub reporter at the time, serving three newspapers with a service that almost earned me a living.

William Hopkin - Alderman – J.P. - County Councillor - Mayor and a heart as big as a whale.

It is a long way back, but well worth the effort. Willie said when he died, the real name of Lady Chatterley would die with him. I beg to differ, but more of that later. Born in 1862, he was in his 90th year when he died. We're talking old men here.

Along with other children of his era he had to pay fourpence a week for lessons at school. Any child who couldn't raise the wind was sent home. He joined the local Wesleyan Chapel and organised meetings with local speakers, but was thrown out for allowing clapping in church. Let's move on, for Pete's sake. He formed the habit of holding meetings in his house- a sort of open forum, where all comers could hold forth on religion, politics, education, what-have-you.

When D. H. Lawrence heard that here was a captive audience, he naturally poked in his nose. Here he found the life-long friends, Willie and his wife Sallie. They were to introduce him to many of the well-known labour leaders of the day.

This grounding was to colour everything that Lawrence wrote in his battle against the hoity-toity-that being the 'landed' few and the pit owners.

On his local walks Lawrence would go out of his way to meet the gamekeepers and the wood-men and argue with them as to who had the right to be there.

Willie had introduced him and encouraged him in his own great love for anything which grew or flew, and both were there to fight their corner for anything from the song thrush to the hawk.

Willie's simple attitude was suited particularly to Eastwood. The small town lived on coal-quite literally. They paved their paths with slack, heated their houses, died for it, and the miners sucked it down pit to ease their thirsts, not having a deal of money for anything else.

Willie stamped his honest authority on Eastwood, which gave rise to many stories, some true, some apocryphal, some shamelessly using him to associate themselves with Lawrence.

As a J. P. On the bench during the Great War, a local poacher was brought before Willie for selling hares, acquired from the land belonging to the local squire. Evidence was laid before him of the poacher hawking them round the pits. Hares and other wild creatures were not specifically mentioned in the meat rationing rules.

Willie spoke up from the magisterial bench. 'I wish he had brought one to me. I'd have bought it. Case dismissed.'

He was a great one for speaking at the school prize-giving ceremonies. As a reporter I usually attended these functions.

'You may,' (he always started with the same words) 'not believe this, but I was once a boy myself.'

There was a disbelieving roar from the pupils.

He was somehow ageless-small, grey, and seemingly not of this world, speaking with an authority beyond the reach of ordinary mortals.

He wrote a big column for the local newspaper, the Eastwood and Kimberley Advertiser- 'Rambling Notes.' He told me that he had written this column for the last fifty years and never received a penny payment.

His wife Sallie was very proud of him. She confided in me that he never swore. 'Not even small words.' That would be four letter words today, I assume.

But I recall a tale he used very often. He was on a night out with some other councillors and having had a few he was having a pee round the back of the premises. It was raining and a down-pipe was gushing its water round his feet.

'Are you ready?' One of his friends shouted.

'I think I'm pissing myself to' Willie looked up 'death,' he responded.

No account of Willie can take place without mentioning D.H.Lawrence, so I must return to Lady Chatterley who is the subject of a new book on Lawrence written by Professor John Worthen: Emeritus Professor of Lawrence studies at Nottingham University, and probably the greatest living authority on this subject.

Now Lawrence himself was very cagey on the subject, confining his remarks to: 'There is a lot of Frieda in Lady C.'

A few facts therefore wouldn't come amiss.

Willie thought that Lady C must be Ottoline Morell, or perhaps Lady Asquith, but the Arkwrights of Sutton Scarsdale Hall must come into the reckoning. Joseph Arkwright fell from a horse and broke his back.

He became impotent, which gave Lawrence the horrors. He dwelt on this until he used the situation in his work.

Lawrence was unable to invent fictional characters and so had to use events from real life -and real people. He said that to be able to invent fictional plots and people, one would need to have a very devious mind, and he would have none of it.

This is what got him into trouble with friends and neighbours. He used their names and experiences with shameless honesty, and objections were raised. He was not liked in Eastwood. He thought that whatever Willie could - he could do.

There were no paparazzi in those days to chastise him, so he just ploughed on. To this day, the first thing the media dive into is: 'Why didn't Eastwood take to their 'Favourite Son?' It is still so.

If there had been no court trial about Lady C, then Lawrence would undoubtedly have been a very back number in Eastwood.

They are more: 'Wham, Bam, Thank you Mam! - still interested in the subject, but not so in your face.'

Let's go back to Willie, and who was Lady Chatterley. I have had the benefit of the later years on this subject so I say to his ghost; 'You were wrong, Willie.'

Lawrence had a sort of vendetta against the Barber family who were the local mine owners and landlords. Barber and Walker had a strangle-hold on the whole area, and this sort of ate into Lawrence's simple soul. He wasted no opportunity to have a dig at them. In his many works of fiction, or indeed perhaps function, he had his sly digs. The Barbers have mainly died out now, but Lawrence did not live to see it. He dealt with it in his own way. In several of his major works he puts in very thinly disguised members of the Barber family.

One has only to be local to know the facts behind many of the events he writes about. He stirs them up with places and names that are a frustrated endeavour to name and shame, but stops short of actually doing that.

Strangely enough he never mixes Willie into the cake, I think Lawrence put Willie on a different planet - a different plane of thought that could not be in his brain at the same time as his darker thoughts. Perhaps he thought he had created enough trouble for his heirs already. He knew the book was trouble. H.G. Wells' wife often did his typing, but would not touch Lady C. He hid it in a drawer for two years and Freida said she could feel it throb every time she walked by.

Enough of Lady Chatterley. This is about Willie - with his clean and kindly nature. But just one last comment, I had the benefit of talking to several of the managers of outlying farms owned by Major Barber, also to the widows after the farmers' deaths.

The Major gave some pretty broad hints that he knew who the book was all about, in one case picking up a copy of it and striking out 'Lady Chatterley' and writing in the name of his mother who was the untitled 'Lady' of the period. Sorry Willie.

Willie carried on with his good work, helping everybody from the vicar to the 'nightsoil' men who emptied the pan lavatories. A euphemism to beat them all.

Sallie died in 1921 and eventually he remarried-Olive-who was just as good to him as Sallie, and carried on with the Sunday evenings, even after Willie's death. It was never quite the same.

Young people came and sat at Olive's feet, but Willie's ghost was there, somehow casting his presence over the proceedings.

He had fairies, angels, and all sorts of things that you could never see. I don't mean to say, like Mark Twain, 'whose education had not been interfered with by too much learning, 'it was just that Willie had an 'Eastwood' heart and soul-mining in the blood and in the pay packets. He never really grew up-thank goodness.

He wrote some pretty good poetry but never broke through into the upper echelons, as he would have wished. When he died he donated piles of Lawrence's works to Eastwood Library.

There rests his poetry along with other precious works that are guarded closely.

Sleep well Willie. A lot of secrets died with you, about Lady Chatterley. Not your sort of world, really.

P. Press Note:

Leslie Williamson was born in Eastwood in 1924. His father, who had fought and been injured in the first world war, had to take whatever work he could find in order to feed his wife and three children, of two sons and a daughter, born profoundly deaf. As an adolescent, Leslie Williamson worked as a laundry boy, collecting and delivering washing, ran errands for a local engineering firm, and also found work on the shop floor at Aristoc, a hosiery business. With the coming of the Second World War he joined the R.A.F. and was eventually posted to Malaya. Peace, however, did not bring the demobilisation he expected.

Instead, his squadron was ordered to Indonesia because the Indonesians refused to allow the Dutch back in to recommence the administration of their country.

However, in Leslie's own words, 'to all those Indonesians wanting their freedom we became the Dutch, it was like being an American soldier in Iraq.' A bomb exploding near by cost him the hearing in his right ear and he was invalided back to Lincolnshire before eventual discharge.

Once on civvy-street he rejoined Aristoc, in which business he rose to become a manager, and having taught himself short-hand, also found work as a reporter for local newspapers.

He began to write fiction and poetry, and among his published work are three novels: *The Crowded Cemetery: Death of a Portrait:* **and** *Jobey*,

which is set in 1926, during the General Strike, and which Methuen paper-backed at the time of the 1984-5 Miners Strike.

It has recently been re-published in a large print edition.

(Leslie Williamson is, in addition, the author of the verse sequence: ***D.H. Lawrence and the Country he Loved,*** **and** *Bread for All,* The Ulverscroft Foundation, 2002) which he describes as 'A dramatic interpretation of the Pentrich Uprising,' that forlorn effort by early nineteenth century Derbyshire miners to overthrow the government, and which led to execution, transportation (the largest prison in Australia is called Pentrick) and prompted among other things Shelley's great essay on Liberty.

A dramatic version of *Bread for All*, adapted for the stage by its author, is to be presented by a local school later this year. In the late autumn of 2004, Leslie Williamson's three short plays on Byron played to packed audiences in Eastwood.

John Lucas: Pennyless Press

The Breach House

This potted history of 'The D.H. L. Breach House' kindly contributed by Dr. David Amos of the D. H. Lawrence Society.

D.H. LAWRENCE HOUSE in the Breach, Eastwood   1/2
The 'Sons and Lovers' Cottage - History (1972 – 2011)

Honorary Deedholders : Dr James Roberts (U.K.) & Dr Douglas Sasse (U.S.A.)

Purchased on behalf of the Canadian Association for Young Writers. Subsequently run by Wirral O.W.L. and the DHL House Purposes Committee now bequeathed to the Merseyside Erasmus Foundation

Restoration by Nottingham architect, Henry Mein and Holmes Brothers, builders.
(although derelict and despite minor fire damage, both the exterior and interior of the property were virtually intact from its Victorian past)

Retired miners from the Barber-Walker Company volunteered valuable labour

Opened as a World Meeting House for the Arts, Industry and Education

Assistance from Eastwood and later Broxtowe Councils, Notts Building Preservation Trust, University and Polytechnic of Nottingham, Oxford University, East Midlands Arts, City of Nottingham and Eastwood Libraries, the D.H. Lawrence Society and many local well-wishers including voluntary gardeners

Visits by people from all over the world including authors, academics, actors, film and theatre people and Frieda von Richtofen's daughter.

Meeting-place for Eastwood Writers and Eastwood Arts

Field Experience Centre for American university students who did voluntary work overseas and field studies as an alternative to military service during the war in Viet Nam.

Home-from-home for actors from Nottingham Playhouse, including the theatre dog whose fate, some say, inspired the demise of the hapless poodles in "A Fish Called Wanda".

Publication of 'The Young Writers' Review' with poetry contributions from schools and colleges in 26 countries. Two of the poems won major literary awards.

Selection as a featured building for the European Architectural Heritage Year

Setting for major films and several television documentaries

A hospitality centre during D.H. Lawrence Centenary and other Festivals

Guardian Writer of the Year as writer-in-residence

Live broadcasts by Radio Four and the B.B.C. World Service

Annual prizes for young writers

Free Lawrence-Byron weekends for university and college students

Support for the late Leslie Williamson's innovative writing programmes for 'lifers' in Nottingham Prison; through Alex Baxter for the University of Nottingham's Tools for Self-Reliance in Africa group; through John Baxter of the Wilfred Owen Association,

Birkenhead; through Mike Hewitt for the Chernobyl Children's Lifeline; through Kay Scarratt for the Charles Scarratt Merseyside Schools' Music Awards; through Henry Worsley for The Shackleton Foundation; through James Roberts for Wirral O.W.L.

and the Merseyside Erasmus Foundation; through Frank Moran for the Athenaeum

Creative Writing Awards.

The garden was filmed for television programmes and featured in gardening magazines

D.H. Lawrence rose propagated from the briar mentioned in 'Sons and Lovers'

This ancient plant was destroyed when gas-fitters without permission were searching for a gas supply that did not exist.

Weekend visit by Le President du Conseilleurs Generaux to Liverpol Erasmus students and Language Assistants on s field trip in Eastwood.. Le President was so impressed by what he saw that he delayed his departure and had to obtain special permission for his late appearance for a meeting at Chequers with Prime Minister Margaret Thatcher.

J.K.R.

August, 2011

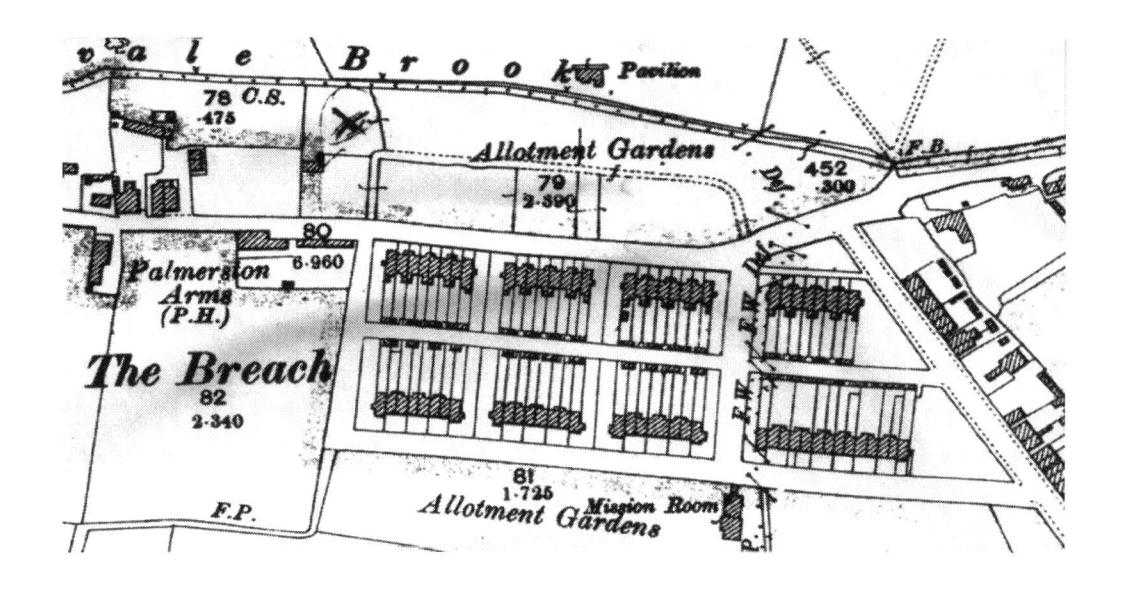

"it was a little less common to live in the Breach"

This is the house known to all readers of Lawrence as the setting for "The Bottoms" in "Sons and Lovers". In 1887, the Lawrence family - by this time seven of them - moved here from Victoria Street and stayed until 1891. Since it was an end house with additional space, they paid an extra sixpence rent each week. As Lawrence later recalled, "it was a little less common to live in the Breach."

In "Sons and Lovers" the reader is entertained with much rich information about Eastwood and the day-to-day life of a mining family. It is within the fictional setting of this house that we learn of common issues such as the creative weekly struggle to make ends meet and the strong influence of the coal mining industry to the area. The kitchen of this house is also the place where, in the novel, many scenes depicting the often-difficult relationships within the Lawrence family are played out.

You've just missed Mister Lawrence, he's gone out t'settle pit dust!

The Breach House fire range, it would have been beautifully black-leaded by the miner's wife

The D.H.L. Breach wash-house

Harry Riley's note and introduction to the Eastwood Writers Group:

The late Leslie Williamson was once Chairman of the Eastwood Writers Group: he published The Eastwood Anthology in 1998, a collection of poems and short stories.

The group is still flourishing strongly. Owing to other commitments, I am a lapsed member, but I still like to keep in touch. In fact I participated in their latest anthology which is available from Amazon.

Introducing the book, entitled **'A Window Into Eastwood Writers Group'** Chair: at the time: Dianne Rasmussen says: 'A Window Into Eastwood Writers Group is an anthology, a collection, a garland of our work. We are a diverse group who share a love of writing. We have produced this book to showcase our work and to encourage ourselves and others to keep writing and improving. Some of our poems and stories will make you smile and maybe a few will produce the retort: 'I never thought of that.' Some of us are published authors, others are trying to become, published, but we all love to write. We hope you enjoy reading our book and that it encourages you to try letters, novels, diaries or anything more than a shopping list. We are based near Eastwood Nottinghamshire, the home of D. H. Lawrence, and one day one of us may be as well known as he. The rest of us will write at home and meet every Tuesday at Brinsley Parish Hall to critique our efforts.'

Dianne Rasmusson Chairman of Eastwood Writers Group 2014.

'A 'chairman' is not necessarily a man, any more than a catastrophe is always caused by a cat, although both can be.'

Earlier Eastwood Writers Anthology with intro by Chairman Leslie Williamson.

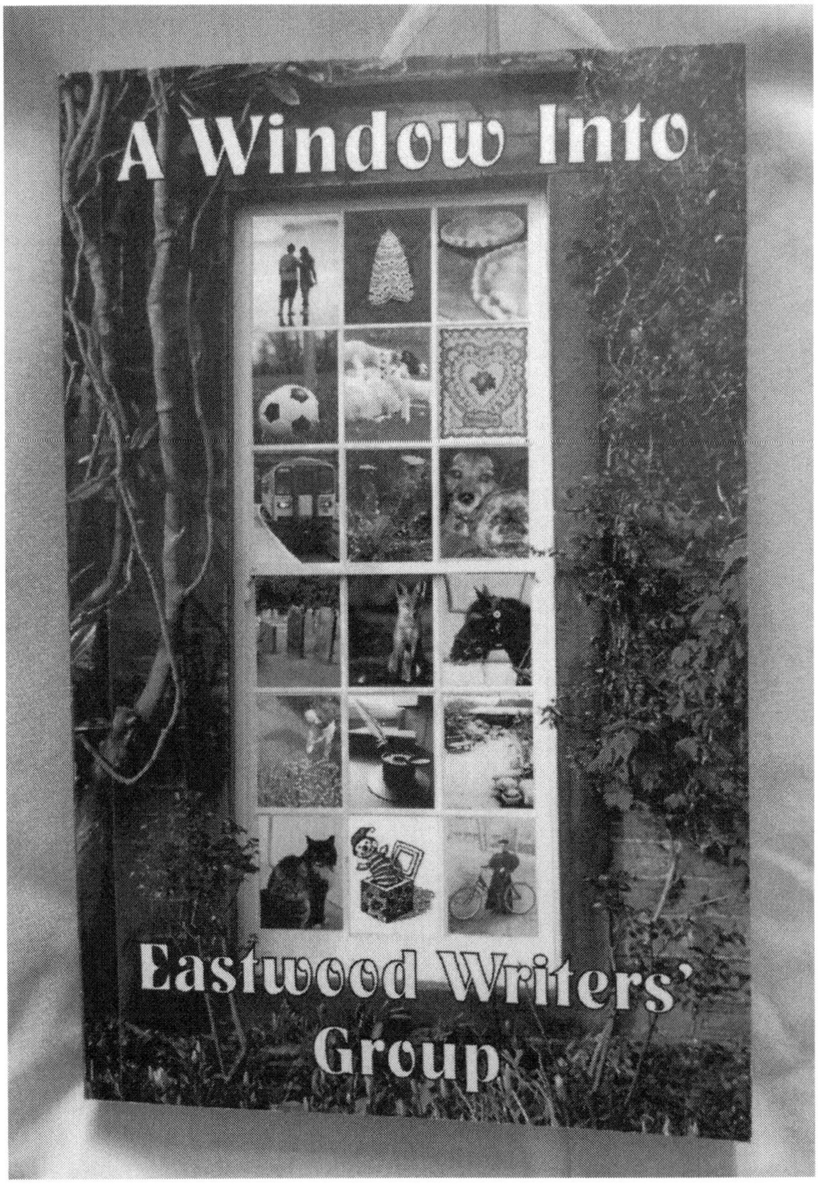
A Window Into
Eastwood Writers'
Group

Chapter 7: Anniversary Archives

Harry's note:

In volume one I wrote about The Baptist Church situated on Percy St. Eastwood and it's impending 140th anniversary of early 2016.

This has now happened and Brian and I went along to meet Reverend Nick Price and to view his church archive display.

A room in the church has been set aside to display dozens and dozens of photographs and articles, going back over many decades of church worship.

These archives have been lovingly collated into various categories by dedicated followers of the Baptist faith.

Stained glass window at Percy Street. Baptist Church

The Archives Display at Percy Street Baptist Church

The archives were also on view inside the church entrance and knowing very little about the Baptists, several articles caught my eye.

One of them was headed: **The Historic Chapel at Monksthorpe.**

I was intrigued, and even more so when I was informed the Reverend Bryan Keyworth, who lives at Eastwood, is the Baptist Minister in charge of it, on behalf of The National Trust.

I later asked Bryan if he would care to share a few words about Monksthorpe Chapel and he has contributed an extract from the book about memories of Monkthorpe:

'A 90 year Family Connection'

Arthur Keyworth was a Baptist lay preacher. He and his family were living in Skegness. In 1924, he had taken a service in the Monksthorpe Chapel. While showing some people around after the service he had a heart attack, collapsed and died in the grounds close to the chapel door.

A few years later, his son Harold began to preach, visiting Baptist churches in Lincolnshire, Nottinghamshire and Cambridgeshire. During the war he was a Civil Defence officer, and afterwards moved to Nottingham where there were family roots. He earned his living as a Master Decorator, but also became Lay Pastor at Newthorpe, close to Eastwood.

In 1957 Harold was invited to become the Lay Pastor of Burgh-le-Marsh and Monksthorpe Churches in Lincolnshire, which functioned together. He had a great love of Monksthorpe and during his time there he repainted the church inside and out.

Harold served there until he died during a Sunday School Anniversary Service at Burgh in 1960: his ashes are placed at the spot where his Father died.

After his death, the church members at Burgh asked his wife, Ada, if she would consider becoming their Lay Pastor. She was already a seasoned Lay Preacher and worked hard for the Girl's Life Brigade, becoming a Major! She served Burgh and Monksthorpe for 8 years, until her death. Her ashes were placed with her husband's.

When Harold started his ministry at Monksthorpe he was unable to fulfil a preaching commitment on Easter Day as he already had a preaching engagement at his previous Church at Newthorpe.

So he sent his son: Bryan, who had begun lay-preaching. He took his girlfriend Janet to sing a solo and they have been going there ever since!

They married in 1960 and were distressed when the Chapel was closed in 1972 due to damage from the roots of a large tree. Bryan pestered the East Midlands Baptist Association about the state of Monksthorpe and he was offered the chance of doing something about it. By now Bryan was an ordained Baptist Minister and during his leisure moments worked hard for several years to try to save the chapel. Others helped of course, but it was an uphill task. Eight years of negotiating with the National Trust saw the chapel handed over, the Friends of Monksthorpe entrusted with the ordering of worship, and Bryan appointed their local minister-although he lives eighty miles away in **Newthorpe!**

Bryan's son is a Baptist minister working at the Baptist Union Head Office, and a grandson is now a Baptist minister in Manchester. The Keyworth family's service in Baptist churches and connections with Monksthorpe span an amazing five generations.

Another flyer, of which Nick Price kindly loaned me a copy, was published by Bassetlaw Christian Heritage/Bassetlaw District Council and concerned **Thomas Helwys**-founder of the Baptist denomination and Pioneer of Religious Liberty for All. His death in Newgate Prison was to be marked on 12th March 2016 at 'The Well' Hospital Road. Retford Notts., as it would be the 400 years anniversary of this man's death.

Thomas was from a north Nottinghamshire family. His family held lands at Askham, at Saundby and in Lincolnshire. Thomas Helwys was friendly with the puritan John Smyth and helped finance the escape from persecution of The 'Pilgrims' to the Netherlands in 1608.

That point particularly interested me, as I had once tried to join the Friends of The Pilgrim Fathers, but had been informed membership was only open to proven descendants.

Anyway, to return to Thomas. He founded the English Speaking Baptist-denomination-the largest single Christian group in the USA and I think it is well worth recording the basic facts, with nearly 50 million Baptists worldwide. If that is not an achievement, then I don't know what is.

The Baptist faith only became legal in England in 1691.

So what did Thomas Helwys die for?

I now understand he was the first Englishman to explicitly state that people of any religion-Christian, Jew, or Muslim, should be free to exercise their faith without government interference.

Not a lot to ask you might think, but nevertheless they hanged him for declaring it. How many of us would have crumbled and backed down, when faced with that ultimate threat of death, I wonder.

As a youngster, with not really religious-minded parents, I was nevertheless obliged to attend church on a Sunday.

I believe it was more for the neighbours' benefit than for my own enlightenment, but it was one day a week when we had to scrub-up and wear our best clothes, and no climbing trees.

So, with a group of pals, boys and a few girls, we decided we would obey our parents and attend church as required, but as there were quite a few churches and chapels in and around our district we would try them all alternately, to see which was most child friendly. The best, most interesting ones were evangelist missions, where even the elders seemed to enjoy themselves, and when the preacher cried out in religious fervour: 'Who'll come to Jesus and be saved?'

We were among the first to raise our arms up high. Needless to say we received prizes, invariably books that I'm ashamed to say we would often trade in to our more enlightened friends after school.

However there was one book which I could not bring myself to part with and it was entitled: **Twelve Brave Boys,** and which I wish I had kept. Which brings me to the point of this long-winded tale. I am sure one of the 'Brave Boys' was a certain Thomas Helwys. Another one was William Wilberforce, he who fought to abolish slavery.

✥✥✥

Percy Street Baptist Church Eastwood, built by volunteers, has a fully tiled sunken bath and they regularly fill their Sunday services with worshippers.

The church is very much an integral part of the community with various groups using the premises for a wide variety of leisure activities.

Mrs. Jean Duckworth is one of the Percy Street Baptist archivists and is the widow of Jack Duckworth, who died on 25th March 1994.

Jean was present on the day we visited Revd. Nick Price to view the Church Archives, before they are carefully packed away again for safekeeping.

Jean lent me a book – a biography she had published about the life and times of her husband, the man who friends called 'Jumping Jack' and appropriately enough, this is the book title.

It is of course a Christian book with the sub-title 'Soldiering on for God.' However Jack's pastoral, evangelical and divine healing ministry (to quote Jean's own words from the book,) took him worldwide, after serving in the forces during world war two. And this is where my main interest in reading his story lay. I chose to read it as a very interesting and inspiring travel book. I am sure avowed and practicing Christians will get much more from this book than I could, but I still found plenty to interest me in his fascinating travels around the globe.

It is a superb tribute to a great humanitarian, written in a fast and pacey style by Jean, which is never boring and is accompanied by some attractive pics, as he crossed continents on his life-mission.

Some people may remember Jean Duckworth from her previous contributions to **'A Century Remembered'** By Michael Bennett- Reminiscences of everyday life in the Eastwood area.

Published by Eastwood Historical Society. A beautifully printed book, containing over 200 illustrations and specially produced and edited by Michael Bennett for the 2000 Millenium.

Jean Duckworth (nee Leverton) and her twin brother; Ian were born in 1941. They attended Greasley Beauvale School and Eastwood County Secondary School (Walker Street.)

Jean married Lancastrian, Jack Duckworth in 1971 and in 1979/80 accompanied him on a World Preaching Mission.

Jean had three books of Christian Poetry published in the 1970's and in year 2000 published **'Jumping Jack'** (*Her husband's biography and his nickname, acquired through his boundless energy, and ability to bounce back up again, after a setback.*)

Jean is a member of the **'Word Weavers'** writing group of Eastwood.

Here, for poetry lovers, is a taste of her poignant verse:

'Eastwood Cemetery'

I know a place where daisies grow
Among the grasses green
Where tears are shed and harsh winds blow
And peace commands the scene

It is the door to Heaven's home
It's entrance, dark, concealed
For you went through and I alone
Stood in the daisy field

Those small white guardians of the mound

Where you and I did part

In simple splendour, still are found

Cocooning you sweetheart

Jean Duckworth

(In memory of her husband: Jack)

Harry Riley's note:

The next poem Jean shares with us, touches on this subject of being aware of the things that really matter in life, rather than material possessions, and evokes for me, personal memories of strolling along by the sea at Lindisfarne (Holy Island) Northumberland. Of a holiday at Loch Linnhe Scotland, and of reading a memorable book about otters: **'Ring of Bright Water'** by Gavin Maxwell.

A man who had nothing and yet really had it all, with peace and contentment, until the double edged sword of fame and fortune came along and ruined his peaceful Scottish island sanctuary of *Camusfearna*, and taking his solace away.

Such can be the power of poetry.

Contentment

Content to know that I am me

To feel the love that comes from thee

To grasp the pebble in my hand

And not to reach for those beyond

the water's edge

For they are slippery and wet

Half hidden in dark sea-weed's net

They beckon with mysterious lure

And of my safety I'm not sure

at water's edge

Content Dear Lord, please let me be

with all the things you've given me

And not to strive with anxious mind

The larger, brighter stones to find

at water's edge

Jean Duckworth

(inspired on a holiday on Fetlar, Shetland Isles.)

The Proposal

Hubert and Sally were sweethearts
They'd been courting for many years,
But Hubert was happy to let things go slow,
Which had poor Sally in tears.

She steered him towards the jewellers,
But he seemed to walk by,
Oblivious to her silent pleadings
Took interest in birds flying by

When would he propose, she thought dreaming
Of wedding Bells, churches and rings,
But he, unaware of her feelings
Had his mind always on other things.

And then came the day of excitement,
He said he'd got something to say
But she'd have to go on a journey
And then he would show her the way.

She felt sure this was the proposal,
So she put on her Sunday Best
And together they walked through the Church Yard
Up to the Chapel of Rest.

He led her into the Cemetery
To a very significant spot,
And proudly with pointed finger
Showed her his family plot

With bated breath she waited,
The proposal was strange but sincere,
Sal, these are my ancesters,
Would you like to be buried here?
Jean Duckworth *(written from a true story)*

Jumping Jack
Soldiering on for God

A Biography of
JACK DUCKWORTH
by
Jean Duckworth

Jumping Jack is a great inspiring story and travel book

*Jack and Jean Duckworth arriving outside the gates
of Buckingham Palace, for their invitation to
The Queen's Garden Party: July 15th 1986*

Chapter 8 'Entertainment'

The Arcadian Band and Remembering Maurice Price.

Even the Mascot has to stand to attention in the presence of the Grenadier Guards

'Back in the late 1970's we sat in the Lord Raglan pub on a lad's night out.

We met a man who we all got to know as Mr. Price. He had a drink with us and told us not to waste money on drink and women, we were all single at the time.

He told us the Arcadian's were re-forming after he'd had a meeting with some of the war Arcadians, and it was decided the young people of Eastwood needed something to do.

Hence the Arcadians started. With a strong marching band we would go to practice twice weekly, at the Walker Street School.

Later it was to be anywhere else Mr. Price could beg.

We went out on a John Clarkes Bus every weekend all over the country, entering competitions in which we scooped the championship, making Mr. Price and ourselves very proud.

There was not another band, thanks to Mr. Price's dedication, that could touch us.

Some of Mr. Price's quirky sayings: 'Shoulders back and chests out!' –

'It's only rain and you won't rust!' And when he shouted '**ATTENTION!**' You daren't breathe, but it worked.

On one of the first parades someone said there was a hole in the ground, which he fell into, and stopped playing his drum.

Mr. Price's words were: 'you should continue playing until you hit the bottom.'

Being an ex-Grenadier Guard, Mr. Price made sure the Arcadians were marching through Eastwood Town during the annual Remembrance Day Services, as it was always a special day for him.

All we can say is he was a true gentle giant, who left so many memories: Thanks Mr. Price!'

The tall Mr. Price and the Grenadier Guards inspecting the Assembled Band of The Arcadians.

Arcadians proudly marching through the town

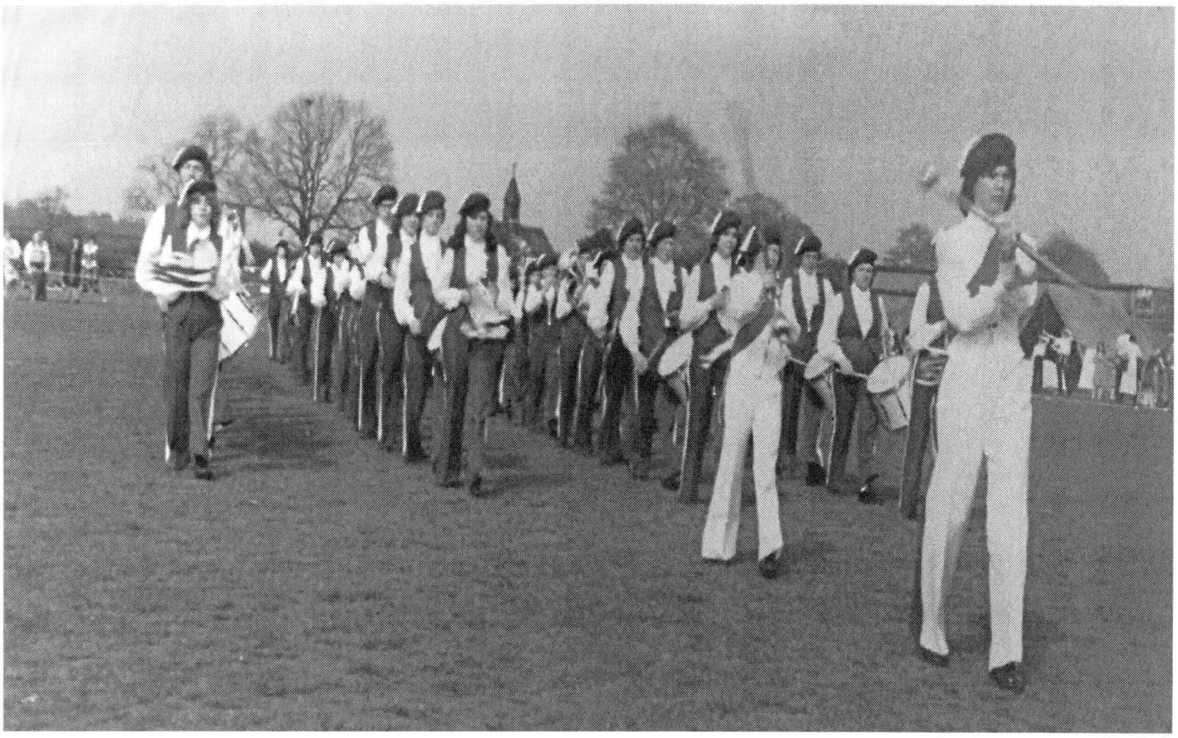

Arcadian Bandsman Ian Dunstan

Ian on his wedding day. Being saluted by the Arcadians

Millside Hospital Radio and 'Eastwood Chapter & Verse Community Group.'

What, you may ask, has a hospital radio to do with a book about Eastwood?

Well, it happened like this; my first contact with Kingsmill Hospital and Millside Radio was when, along with a group of other like-minded local people, including two Eastwood Councillors and the Head of Eastwood Comprehensive School, we formed 'Eastwood Booktown Development Group.'

During this time we came up with the idea for a summer fete, which we called 'Eastwood Expo and Booktown Bonanza,' (a one day family event.)

Beauvale Abbey was the chosen venue, kindly provided by Abbey Farm owners: Mr. and Mrs. Whyte.

In order to get the best possible coverage, we advertised in the press and with posters, and informed Millside Radio, of which I had recently become a volunteer: daily 'Reflections' presenter.

Radio Station Manager: Peter Wilson-Neasom, Sue Smith, and Station Programme Controller: Trevor White, came along to Beauvale Abbey on the day, bringing their radio mascot: Millie Bear, to do a walk-about in the grounds. They also did a recording for hospital patients and the Internet and displayed their large banner.

We recorded approx 800 people attending the Bonanza, not bad for a somewhat cloudy day with only occasional sunshine and an out-of-the-way location.

The Event was opened by Eastwood's Mayor: Councillor Hazel Charlesworth.

Later when world star, singer/songwriter: Jackie Trent became Patron of our Booktown Group, she came to Eastwood over a weekend and Brian Fretwell put her and husband Colin up in his bungalow. We took her to visit Durban House and she met students and teachers from Eastwood Comprehensive school. This meeting was featured in the Nottingham Post and following this, Millside Radio invited Jackie along to the studio to record her life story and involvement with Eastwood Booktown group. I met her at Kingsmill Hospital, as she returned, from her home in Spain, along with Colin, her Nottingham-born, ex-policeman husband.

Sadly this recording was to be the penultimate one she was to make before her sudden death.

However, Millside Radio later joined Eastwood Chapter and Verse Community Group for 'The Battle of Waterloo Bicentenary Memorial Service,' held at Cossall Church of St. Catherine, and led by Reverend Dr. Andy Lord.

Millside Radio brought along their 'Outside Broadcast Camera' and Radio Presenter Trevor White interviewed several of the specially invited guests including principal guest: The Lord Lieutenant of Nottinghamshire: Dr. Jas. Bilkhu.

Millside Radio's Peter Wilson-Neasom and Sue Smith were also present. As were East Midland Television Camera Crew and Programme Presenter: Quentin Raynor.

Several Mayor's and Councillors were also in attendance, including Councillor Mrs. Sue Bagshaw: Mayor of Broxtowe, and Councillor Keith Longdon, Mayor of Eastwood. Nottinghamshire Police Commissioner: Paddy Tipping and Eastwood Town Clerk: Chris Thompson, who led a joint Commemorative walk to Cossall Village, on behalf of Notts Guided Walks, and Eastwood Chapter and Verse Community Group, who helped organise the event, along with Rev. Dr. Lord and his church parishioners, Cossall and Awsworth Councillors.

Since then, Chapter and Verse group has been involved in several Millside Radio special projects including Memories of World War Two and 'Monday Washday' (involving personal memoirs by Eastwood Writers Group.) Plus a virtual Dementia-Memory Café, and a one act play for radio: 'Twice Loved,' recorded with the Millside Players.

Incidentally, a recording of this production has been played, and well received by The Friendship Club of St. Mary's Church Eastwood.

Kingsmill Hospital is being taken over by Nottingham University Hospital Trust, which runs both Nottingham Queens Med, and The City hospital, so the future for Millside Radio is hopefully going to continue to be as bright and rewarding for the community as their distinguished, 25 year past.

Website:www.millsideradio.co.uk: tel:01623737 737

A Millside Radio Fund Raising event at Kingsmill Hospital.

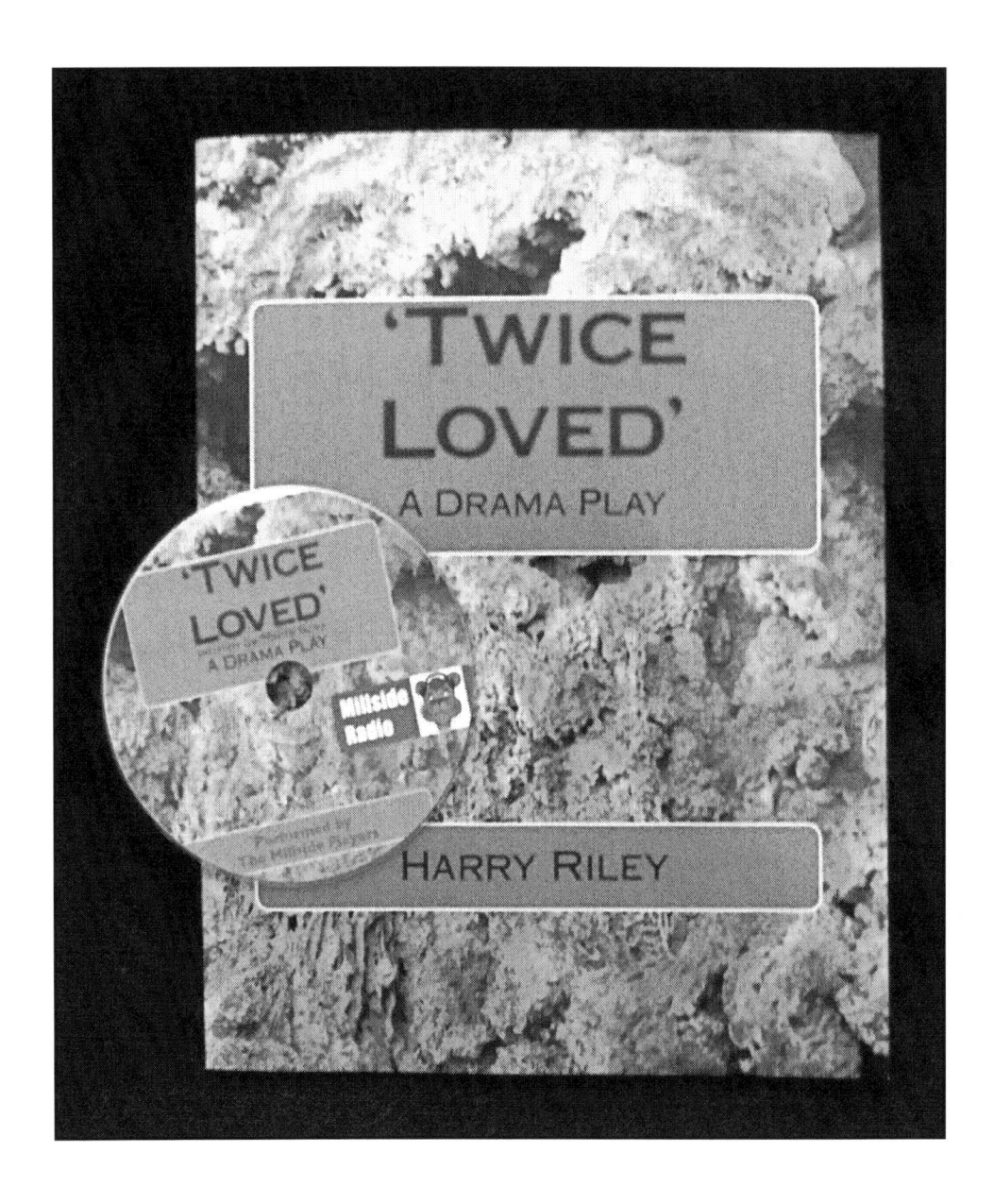

Chapter and Verse joint venture with Millside Radio Drama play and CD produced by Trevor White and performed by the Millside Players

Murals in the 'Street' Corridor of Kingsmill Hospital

'Have you got any gum chum?' *Wartime memories of when this Mansfield infirmary became a hospital for wounded American Servicemen.*

FIRST UNITED STATES ARMY
★★★★ HOSPITAL IN ENGLAND
GENERAL
No. 30
HOSPITAL
"OVERPAID, OVERSEXED AND OVER HERE!"
AMERICAN BASEBALL
THE CAUCIANS DANCE BAND

30TH GENERAL HOSPITAL OF THE UNIVERSITY OF CALIFORNIA
By December 1942 there were 50 officers, 75 ANC (ancillary) and 319 EM (enlisted men). The organisation occupied one enlisted, one nurses and two officers barracks, with four wards (enlisted barracks) and utilised the main kitchen, one mess hall and one combined officers and nurses mess.
GENERAL
No. 30
HOSPITAL

*The late Singer/Songwriter: Jackie Trent
She became Patron of Eastwood
Development Group and visited Durban
House, meeting Town Councilors and
students from Eastwood Comprehensive.
Millside Radio recorded her bio just before
She died.*

....

The Special Battle of Waterloo Bicentenary Service held at Cossall Church.

During my own internet research into 'The Cossall Giants' and their involvement in The Battle of Waterloo, I came across a gruesome but intriguing tale of how the great Scottish Writer: Sir Walter Scott had become friends with John Shaw (The Boxing Cossall Giant, who had heroically fought and died in the battle) and that some short time after 'Waterloo' had himself sought out the grave of John Shaw on the battlefield, and had somehow obtained permission to exhume the body and to take a Bronze Cast of his skull. According to the author of this strange tale, Sir Walter had taken the Scull-Cast home to Abbotsford, his grand house at Melrose in the Scottish Borders and had displayed in for several years for friends and history buffs to marvel at.

As a fan of the great man's writing I wanted to find out for myself if there was any real credence in this story. So having planned to re-visit Northumberland and the Scottish Borders on holiday in 2016, (I found my wife and I taking time out to visit Abbotsford and talking to the curator of this superb museum. incidentally the setting of my previous two murder, mystery novels.)

This pilgrimage was a labour of love, and I wanted to know if their was any real validity in the tale of Scott and his friendship with our local giant soldier of Waterloo.

She was eager to oblige, and not only was it true about the friendship and the author's visit to the Battleground, but John Shaw's body had been exhumed. The only discrepancy was that the skull-cast he brought back was not bronze metal, but a bronze-coloured plastercast.

And there it was!

Still visible for all to see, at one end of the mantelpiece. At the other end of the high stone mantelpiece was a plaster-cast skull of the great Scottish patriot: King Robert The Bruce. Another interesting piece of history from our Eastwood and district vicinity is also displayed in the Abbotsford Museum, and that is The poet Lord Byron's epic Childe Harold and it's third-canto: Battle of Waterloo 'King-making Victory.'

Sir Walter Scott's Abbotsford on the banks of the River Tweed

The contents of Abbotsford are just as Sir Walter left them, and now in the loving care of the trust for all to enjoy.

The plaster-cast of Giant Waterloo Hero 'Life Guardsman Corporal John Shaw' from Cossall Village, displayed at Sir Walter Scott's Abbotsford.

Chapter 9: Sporting, School, Work and Church

Jimmy Loughrey.

(An Appreciation: by Declan Forde)

There are two reasons why Jimmy Loughrey is an iconic figure to many people in Eastwood and the surrounding area and both of them are sport related. In the mid 1960's Jimmy along with Phil Maloney helped to run the youth club attached to "Our Lady of Good Counsel" Catholic Church at Hilltop. From this developed Priory Celtic Football Club, the players of which were mostly altar boys at the church plus some school friends one of whom was Tony Woodcock, the future England International. Jimmy invited some of the parents to assist him in running the club and to instill a rather strict disciplinary code. Fortunately all the young players came from homes of good character so it was easy to maintain the code he set and these standards are still applied to the club to this day.

It is from such humble origins that Priory Celtic is today one of the leading youth football teams in the East Midlands and will be forever Jimmy Loughrey's legacy.

His other sporting connection stems from his founding of the **Eastwood Amateur Boxing Club.** His interest in the noble art came from his own involvement as a professional boxer during which he was the Flyweight Champion of Ireland. His record as a professional can be downloaded on Google simply by inserting Jim Loughrey boxer.

As with his experience of running a football team Jimmy insisted on rules of strict behaviour which was a valuable lesson for those who were members of the club some of whom brought glory to the town of Eastwood through their exploits in the ring.

These days the mention of the name Jimmy Loughrey evokes very pleasant memories for lots of Eastwood residents and it is no surprise that this genial Irishman from Derry in the year 2000 was given a special millennium award to thank him for his efforts on behalf of the youth of Eastwood and beyond.

Harry Riley's note:

After a period of homelessness when Eastwood Boxing Club had to be content to train in the basement/skittle alley of a local pub, a new home was found for them.

This was to be in the Old Pottery building on Church Street Eastwood close by St. Mary's Church and overlooked by the now newly refurbished Devonshire Drive apartments (what was the old Devonshire Drive School).

The Old Pottery building had lain vacant and unloved for years and it was a mammoth task to bring it back into a safe and satisfactory condition. Chris Halpin, Chairman of the boxing club says he is proud of what they have achieved with the building renovation in such a short space of time. All members worked with tremendous enthusiasm, including family support. They had no plumbing or electrics, the floor had to be levelled and the roof leaked.

They worked all hours including weekends and the building was officially opened by Eastwood Town Mayor: Councillor Keith Longdon on August 9th 2016.

Brian Fretwell and I went along to the Open Day on Saturday 24th September to see for ourselves and to take a few pics for this book.

The restoration work has all been internally so far as was entirely necessary. Outside the building is unchanged in appearance and is causing concern to the new apartment holders, particularly the rear aspect which faces their windows.

However, once inside it is evident that a tremendous transformation has taken place and that Eastwood Boxing Club now has a real building to call home.

This Open Day also had another purpose because the Mayor of Broxtowe: Councilor Graham Harvey was here to present a cheque of £1500:00 on behalf of the Borough Council to Chairman Chris Halpin and Club Treasurer Ron Goddard.

Later I spoke to Ron and he told me a little about his involvement with the club and his own interest in the sport of boxing.

Ron, who will be 90 next Birthday, is still very alert and looks remarkably healthy, which must say a lot for his lifelong fitness regime. He tells me he was in the services and Home Fleet, Mediterranean and South Pacific Boxing Champion, fighting 81 amateur and 38 contests as a professional fighter and only lost two bouts. He has been with Beeston and Long Eaton Boxing clubs before becoming Treasurer of this Eastwood club, which had been founded by Jimmy Loughrey over thirty years ago.

He insists that this club is more than just boxing though, as it develops fitness, character and confidence in a youngster, plus positive values.

This was evident as two young lads gave us an impromptu exhibition of skipping inside the ring and another boy was busy pumelling a hanging punch-bag. Ron says that after a period of neglect, schools are again coming around to the realization that amateur boxing is a clean, safe sport and to be encouraged.

EASTWOOD
BOXING CLUB
CONTACT CHRIS - 0779 989 8811 - CALLUM 0783 477 7479

Left to right: Club Chairman Chris Halpin: Club Treasurer Ron Goddard, B.B.C. Mayor-Graham Harvey Cllr, Josie Marsters: Cllr, David Townes

161

Eastwood ABC. ...a home of our own?
Eastwoood Amateur Boxing Club was founded in the 1970's by trainer Jimmy Loughrey. Over the last 40 years we have trained hundreds of boxers, boys, men and the occasional women and girls. We have produced national amateur champions, both male and female, and some have graduated to the paid ranks.
In recent years the clubs survival fell largely on the young shoulders of Callum Hobster. At the age of 18, under the ever present watchful eye of club stalwart and local legend Ron Goddard, Callum became the principal, more often than not lone trainer for the club. Without Callum's loyalty and dedication the club would not have had a future. Over the last couple of years Callum has been joined by Chris Harpin who has bought his vast experience and enthusiasm to the club.

In all our time of operating, the club has never had a home to call it's own. Starting out the club trained at Eastwood Comprehensive school, enjoying the use of their gymnasium, sports field and running track. Due to the development of the gym into a sports centre, the club were forced to find new premises. In stepped the Victory Club. Their basement was used by a skittles and a shooting club (not at the same time it has to be said!) and we had to fit in around them. We had a makeshift ring and somewhere to train, changing our name to Eastwood Victory ABC to reflect this. It was less than ideal though and our search for a suitable home began.

Despite our best efforts and plea's in the local media our search was fruitless. There were high hopes, false starts and the one that got away, but no new premises. We continued to train at the victory club but numbers dwindled and coaches, other than Ron and Callum, came and went. The social climate also meant that the Victory club itself was struggling. Things finally came to a head during a particularly wet month in 2013, not for the first time the basement flooded. But this time was different. Almost a foot deep in water it made our stay untenable.

Salvation came in the form of the Coliseum gym. After a promising start it soon became apparent a new home was needed. Help was sought from Broxtowe Borough Council. With help from Josie Marsters and Keith Longton, we were given valuable advice and were also able to secure some financial help in the form of grants. They were also on the lookout for available premises for us too.

A dilapidated, shell of a youth club lay empty and in a pretty bad state on Church Walk. It had no power or water supply, but Callum and Chris saw an opportunity, a future for our club. A seven year lease was agreed.

Over a period of six months, working weekends and occasional evenings, hundreds of hours of hard work were put in to renovate the building. This included demolishing walls, building work, establishing a power supply and re wiring, plumbing work, installing toilets, sinks and a water fountain. Changing rooms have been created, walls replastered and painted. The floor has been re-concreted and laminate flooring has been laid. This was all done on top of full time work and family life.

The club reopened in it's new home in July 2016. The hard work doesn't stop there though. There is still more work to be done on the building, it will take a lot of time, effort and money to get the rest of the building upto the standard of the gym area. The outside of the building does not reflect the amazing transformation inside.

The club struggles to make the rent based on subs alone. The fees are kept low to make our club accessible to all. In time we will be holding shows, when our boxers are ready to step up to the challenge of competing in the ring. Until then we rely on our own fundraising efforts and the small grants we have been fortunate enough to receive. We are currently looking for sponsors, if this is something you would be interested in, or would like more information about the club, please get in touch at eastwoodboxingclub@hotmail.co.uk

We would love to be able to buy the property outright and secure the future of the club for many years to come, working with the local community to offer a place for youngsters to gain not just boxing skills but life skills such as discipline, determination, self belief and confidence.

We are an ambitious club and know what is achievable through hard work and dedication.
Sara Capill

....

Norman 'Sol' Davis

'Tha didn't need snap, it wore dust what fed yer!'

They were the words of retired Moorgreen Miner: Norman *Sol* Davis, during our conversation at his home in February 2016. Known as *Sol* for most of his working life, Norman was born in Eastwood in 1927 and now, almost nine decades later he still has a tremendous memory of events and people from long ago. He is the oldest man (ex-miner) still living in 'The Buildings.'

(The Barber Walker mining company designed 'The Buildings' in squares for its colliery workers and these brick houses formed the core of Eastwood town.)

Together with his wife Dorothy, who sadly died in 1999, they reared three sons and a daughter, and have twenty two grandchildren.

As a youngster Norman went to British Schools and later to Walker Street School, starting down the pit at seventeen. *'Hey up, I was ganging wi pony and then face cutting, gospel truth, tha didn't need snap, it wore dust what fed yer!'*

And now he's paying for it, with constant painkillers for lung disease. Norman was proud to be number one supporter of Eastwood Town Football Club, affectionately known as the Badgers. The club was founded in 1953 and went on to become professionals in the famous Midland Counties League in 1971, and in 1999 reached the F.A. Cup first round, narrowly losing to Exeter City.

Norman (Sol) Davis

The Badgers have always achieved great things, regularly punching far above their weight, and can claim to have raised the name of Eastwood Town F.C. to stand amongst the greats of football sporting history.

Beth Lee and the Eastwood SKRAISE (Skate Park Project)

'What seems like only yesterday was actually 5 years ago. My peers and I were discussing what we would like to change in our local community; the skate park, in its dangerous and rusty fashion, was the favourite idea. The skate park, situated in Coronation Park, was a popular choice for all ages to socialize and use to practice sporting hobbies, but was also unsafe. This was reason enough to do something about it, and so SKRAISE was created. The project's aim was to collect enough funds for a new, improved and safer skate park to be built for people of all ages and abilities to enjoy.

We rallied support from across the community by setting up a page on social media, asking people to sign a petition and attending various meetings with the councils and the Neighbourhood Watch. But this wasn't all we planned to do - a big group of students from Eastwood Comprehensive School (now Hall Park Academy) came together to begin raising money. Concerts, showcasing students talents, were held, ASDA of Langley Mill allowed us to back pack, and a few local businesses' allowed us to have a collection box in their shops. Before we knew it, the figure was increasing and our applications for further funding from councils and other schemes were successful.

Support was key throughout the project and was never far from reach. Councillor Keith Longdon and Sarah Taylor were there throughout and positive publicity in the local newspapers helped spread our aim across not only Eastwood, but throughout Nottingham.

It seems surreal to visit the park now and see the progress of the build. What was once an idea has become a reality for people across the local community, and visitors to the town to benefit from.

View of the new Skate Park: June 2016

The magnificent new Skate Park seen from above, as adjacent to Coronation Park's Bowling Green.

....

Nine Decades of Life in Eastwood :
By Bill Gregory

My entrance to the world was in 1922 and apart from three and a half years of Second World War two Service, I have spent the whole of my life in Eastwood. To Greasely Beauvale School I went, for my primary education, and later to Eastwood Council School for the secondary one. Times were hard in those days, but in many respects they were happy ones.

At 14 years of age I commenced a five year mechanical apprenticeship at an engineering firm in Sandiacre and at the end of it I knew my future was to be in engineering. The Second World War had commenced by then and I was directed to munition work at Chesterfield, working six nights per week. After about 2 years the travelling got too much so I left and joined the army.

At this time I married my wife Freda and we were to have fifty-four wonderful

years together, she served with the A.T.S while I was abroad.

On my discharge at the end of the war I took a job of early morning shifts at the NCB workshops for five years and did five years of evening study at Derby Technical College to gain engineering qualifications for the future.

The rest of my working life was spent with 19 years at Rolls Royce and 20 years

at Dowty Mining, from where I retired at Christmas 1986 as Works and Production Engineering Manager.

So much for the domestic side of my life. Can I now relate that I have had a very enjoyable cultural one as well.

Over the years I have been involved a lot in community work and local engineering projects. I served on the committee which obtained a grant from

The Lottery for the Broxtowe Sports Hall in Eastwood and in my middle nineties year I am still on the committee for the Broxtowe Partially Sighted Society.

In 1998 I was awarded 'The Freedom of the Borough of Broxtowe' which was a pleasant surprise. I also served 4 years a Broxtowe Councillor and 12 years on Eastwood Town Council.

The year 2004 -2005 was a very happy one for me as Mayor of Eastwood. My wife Freda would have been very proud for me over those two awards, but unfortunately she passed away in 1997.

In conclusion may I say I was asked to cover the domestic and cultural side of my life in this story and write the other side: the sporting side for a later publication. The sporting side covers a 70 years association with Eastwood Town Cricket Club and a lifetime of support for Nottingham Forest F.C. Including 40 glorious years 1950-1990 as secretary of Forest Supporters Club in Eastwood.

Bill Gregory with his presentation award:

Honorary Freeman 'Freedom of The Borough of Broxtowe'

Bill Gregory wearing his chain of office as Town Mayor 2004-2005

Eastwood Community Football Club (CFC) was formed in August 2014 to operate from the former home of Eastwood Town FC. The four Directors who

established the club had a clear vision to create a community based football hub for the benefit of all age groups and / or genders to support the community it serves. In its short history the club has established itself as a function venue and sports facility which have both been invested in heavily to include two refurbished function rooms, toilet facilities and a 3G artificial Wembley size Football Pitch.

The two function rooms are The Pitchside Bar & Lounge which holds 150 together with the 'Erewash Suite' that supports up to 250 people with both available for bookings to include, Weddings, Birthdays, Christenings, Celebration of Life, Anniversary's and Corporate Conferences and functions.

The 3G Pitch is available for ad hoc bookings or for small sided leagues to block book as required as well as hosting the 20 plus Eastwood teams that train and play their football out of the stadium.

The 3G Stadia Pitch is one of a very few across the country and provides unrivalled training and playing facilities in the North Nottinghamshire Football

has been played on Coronation Park for over 60 years and the Eastwood CFC Directors have worked very hard to provide the platform for Football to continue to be played at the site for the next 60 years.

Steve Yardley MIOD

Director: Eastwood CFC & The Venue at Eastwood

....

E: steve.yardley@eastwoodcfc.co.uk

E: steve.yardley@thevenueateastwood.co.uk

T: 01773 432414

M: 07967682245

W: eastwoodcfc.co.uk

W: thevenueateastwood.co.uk

....

Ken Clifford

Harry Riley's note:

In a roundabout way, whilst gathering details of Eastwood St. Mary's Friendship Club, from Janet Shaw, Brian Fretwell, stumbled upon another interesting story: that of Ken Clifford, former Eastwood resident: member of the Friendship Club and now sadly deceased.

Ken's widow: Sheila and their son Stephen had visited the group following his funeral, to present a very welcome legacy, (described as a 'Magnificent Godsend' by St. Mary's Friendship Club, the recipients), to a kindly, supportive and encouraging community group, which in his own words: 'had helped him enjoy life again, after depressive health problems.'

And why is Ken's story so special and interesting in this sporting section? The answer, to those of us who did not know, is that he was a former British Champion Weightlifter. He won cups and trophies in competitions around the world. Before retiring, Ken had been a lorry driver at Moorgreen Colliery.

He ran a training club in purpose built premises at the end of his garden, and was competing well into his seventies before his death at seventy-nine. Friends remember his motto: 'Stay fit, look after your body and do your best!'

What more could anyone ask of us?

Ken Clifford with members of Eastwood Weightlifting club

B.A.W.L.A. AWARD

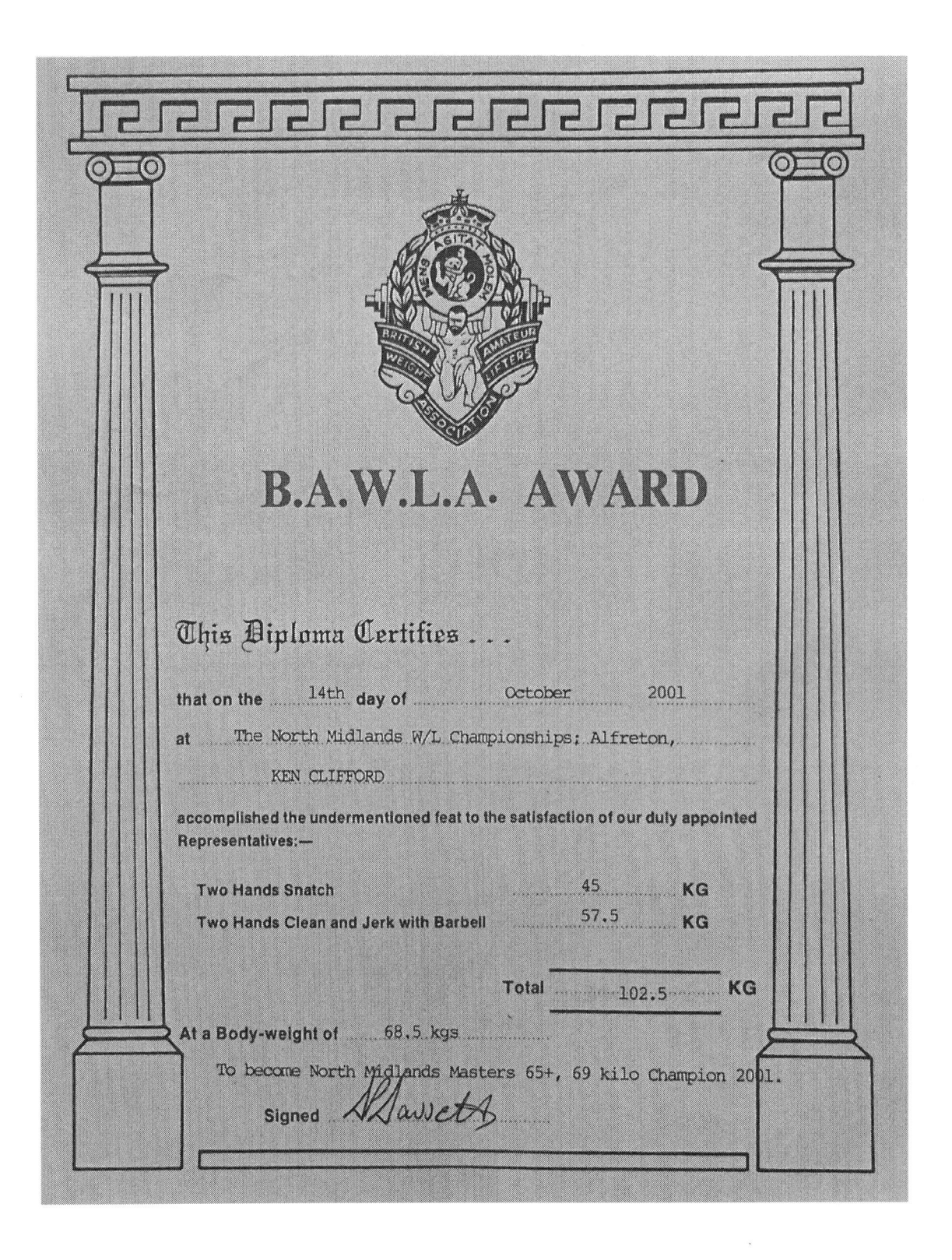

This Diploma Certifies...

that on the 14th day of October 2001

at The North Midlands W/L Championships; Alfreton,

KEN CLIFFORD

accomplished the undermentioned feat to the satisfaction of our duly appointed Representatives:—

Two Hands Snatch	45	KG
Two Hands Clean and Jerk with Barbell	57.5	KG
Total	102.5	KG

At a Body-weight of 68.5 kgs

To become North Midlands Masters 65+, 69 kilo Champion 2001.

Signed

Ken Clifford and young members of Weightlifting Group

Ken was lifting weights into his seventies, and it was said he had his very own elegant style.

⊰⊰⊰

'Janet Shaw continues, with a brief description of **Eastwood St. Mary's Friendship club:**

'...It is unclear when the friendship club first started, as the records were destroyed years ago. It was most likely during the late '80's when the late Colin Dyson MBE first thought of the idea to start a church based friendship group. The Rev and Mrs. Dulcie Sherwood, after retirement, moved to Eastwood and were the first members to join the Club. They joined Colin in leading the club whereby the committee meetings took place along with an AGM, but these days the group is led with a more relaxed attitude.

'In 2002 Colin felt it was time to hand over the leadership to someone else and the then rector Rev Tony Cardwell asked Eve Wharmby and me to take over the leadership, and with fear and trepidation we did!

The group meets at 2pm every Wednesday in the lounge at the back of the church and our subs are just £1:50p per week. We open each week with a hymn, sometimes sing to anyone celebrating a birthday, and a card is presented to that individual, and we feel this is a nice touch.

Any notices are then read out and afterwards we all say a friendship prayer, which was originally written by Colin. We then introduce the speaker who might talk or demonstrate for approximately 45 minutes, followed by tea and biscuits. Members like to chat and return home anytime between 3:30 and 3:45 pm.

'The club has grown steadily over the years. When Eve and I took over there were twenty members which consisted of two ladies in their 90's. The speakers were many and varied and it was a difficult job to organize, as I found out, doing it for more than ten years.

In 2012 Eve had to retire due to ill health. I carried on and by the end of the year Derry Matthews had offered her help and took over the bookings. Another member; Florence Beeney, took over as Treasurer too.

We receive a small grant from Eastwood Town Council, which helps support our funds and Ken Clifford's legacy gift goes towards trips and meals out.

We also present a monetary gift to the church twice a year.

'It is nice to see the club growing and we now have 52 members, our eldest member being Nora Williams at the grand old age of 98.

of course not everyone attends every week, but sometimes the lounge is pretty full. Every one who joins us, the guest speakers too, have commented about the nice atmosphere there is within the club.

So I like to think 'onwards and upwards' and who knows where the club will go over the next few years, but it certainly goes from strength to strength.'

Harry Riley's note: I can second that, having been invited 'guest speaker' at several of their meetings. It is refreshing to see and hear so much enthusiasm from the members.

Members of the St. Mary's Church Friendship Club

....

Still keeping with St. Mary's Church Eastwood there are opportunities for all ages to be part of the Church on Sundays and weekdays.

St. Mary's Toddler Group:

On Tuesday mornings there is the Toddler Group session. While activities are aimed at the under 4's, the children do bring their parents and grandparents with them! So the age range is wide, a few months over 70, and everyone joins in. There are toys: crafts: painting: physical activities: stories and songs, as well as the essential refreshments. They try to celebrate the seasons and major festivals so the children are learning all the time.

St. Mary's has two adjoining rooms that are comfortable and provide adequate but limited space so they can only accommodate about 15 children with adults and helpers. This has its advantages as they can all get to know each other and over the four years they have been running, friendships have been made between some of the mums which are continuing now their children are at school. It is a pleasure to see the children develop and learn to play together, and the leaders of the group feel very privileged to be part of their lives and to be able to support families where they can.

Over the years, several of the children have been baptised in the All Age Service which is held on the first Sunday of the month and to which all are very welcome.

Children and Music in Church:

Children are special and therefore are especially welcome on Sundays at 10: 30 am, along with their parents. There is a children's area equipped with books and toys and seating for adults so the little ones can be occupied while their parents take part in the service. Older children can leave the church for part of the service to enjoy their own teaching and activities and from time to time our older young people take a service themselves which is always refreshing and exciting. Why not join us one Sunday and see for yourself what is going on?

Music is always important in a church service and St. Mary's is fortunate to have a variety of musicians.

They have an accomplished band that plays twice a month, more formal music

on the organ for a 2nd. Sunday Communion service and a piano led group for another service. This means they can sing some of the favourite old hymns as well as exploring the best of the new ones.

St. Mary's band has ventured into the community on several occasions under the title of 'Scary Mary' to entertain at local events with mainly '60's songs, and the two younger members have their own band called: 'Part E' which gigs all over the country.

You can look them up at: **http://www.parteband.com,**

if you wish to know more.

....

Doug Wilcockson

Doug was born in January 1948 at Heanor. When aged 11 he moved to Aldecar, attending Brinsley Infant School, subsequently, attending Langley Mill boys school and Aldecar Sec. Modern, where he captained the football, cricket and cross country teams, later playing for Heanor Town, Awsworth Villa and Old

Heanorians F.C.

Doug has been a member of Eastwood Male Voice Choir, on and off since 1967,

as well as a member of St. Johns Church Choir since the age of 11, and after meeting his wife Valerie he was married at St. Johns, that is where daughters: Vicky and Charlotte were baptised.

Doug has lived in Eastwood for over 44 years, during this time he was Site Manager at Brookhill Leys School for 27 years, where he combined his main job with his passionate interest in sport: not only coaching football, cricket and cross country, but taking teams to compete in all the major tournaments.

Together with Bob Young he helped manage the Eastwood District Team, travelling all over the East Midlands, often on cold and frosty Saturday Mornings. During this time he helped bring about cup winning success for both the boys and girls district teams.

Remaining a familiar face with Eastwood District Sports Association, Doug works at trackside as a Starter Marshall, a role he has undertaken for over 20 years. He was elected as a councillor for both Eastwood Town Council and Broxtowe Borough Council, serving on many committees such as Age Concern: Broxtowe Single Action Group: D.H.Lawrence Forum: Planning and Community Development: Crime Reduction and Eastwood Volunteer Bureau, later being elected Eastwood Town Mayor in 20063/4 and Broxtowe Borough Mayor in 2006/7. Doug has also served as a governor at Brookhill Leys infant and Junior Schools for many years, as well as Brinsley Primary and Langley Mill Infant School and is today still a volunteer for Eastwood Volunteer Bureau.

Doug and his wife presenting flowers to their daughters for their help during his Mayoral Year

Eastwood and District Team of 1997/8

Brookhill Leys Cricket Team of 2001

Eastwood & District Primary School Squad
Winners of Sherwood Forest league and Runners-up
In The County Primary Cup 1997/8
Manager: Bob young and Asst. Manager: Doug Wilcockson

Brookhill Leys School Football Team

Eastwood & District team

County Cup Winners 1996/7

Bob young and Doug Wilcockson

....

Gareth Bowen (Teacher at Devonshire Drive School)

'September 1968. Start of a new chapter of my life: came to Eastwood to begin my teaching career. My first appointment was at Devonshire Drive School (Devo.)

There were five of us from South Wales (Barry Training College) these were David Jones (Kimberley Juniors) : Bob Young, Derek Jones (Beauvale) : Phil James (Brookhill Leys) and Gareth Bowen (Me-Devonshire Drive.)

I was in lodgings on South Street, not too far to walk to school. Came the big day and I approached the school from Church street and it looked solid and foreboding, 'hey ho.' I went up the stairs to the staff room and met my colleagues: so many faces and names etc!

The next step was to meet my class of thirty something - 10-11 year olds. To be honest, just a blank canvas to decipher.

The rest of the day passed as if in a dream, just one memory, how do you spell Ina? Or was it Eina? No, it was Heanor, start of learning curve.

The next stage of my life's journey was football, I didn't know the rules, never played the game, no real interest. Good attributes to be a football teacher in a school with a successful heritage.

The training and organization was largely up to the boys, then the hard bit came, we had to go to play at Jacksdale, Holly Hill, Awsworth etc.

No cars, so we had to get there by bus: but where were all these places?

Yet despite all the trials, the buses were sorted out and we fulfilled our fixtures, then came the last game of the season against Horsendale School. We had only to avoid losing to win the league.

Then the wheels started to come off. By half time we were three nil down. Then thankfully things turned around and in the end we won 4-3 CHAMPIONS!

A good ending to my first year teaching.'

Little did I know that this was the beginning of a forty year love affair with the school, pupils, staff and parents.

…..……………………………………………………………………………………………………..
……

Walker Street School 1933-1972 By Don Chambers

The Hadow Report of 1926 favoured a break in education at the age of 11. Children not selected for Grammer school would attend a senior elementary (modern) school.

Eastwood Higher Council School was thus planned and built at a cost of about £20,000 pounds.

It opened on 9th January1933 with a staff of 15 teachers, 492 pupils including 6 classes for boys, 6 for girls and class sizes of 40 pupils.

Mr. A.H. Scott, who had been head teacher at Greasley Beauvale School since 1930, was appointed head teacher at this new school.

Mr. W. E. Hopkin and Major T. P. Barber considered it to be 'the last word' in elementary education.

The school not only built up a good reputation in sport, but also in music, drama and dance, and competed in local festivals.

Major changes occurred in World War 2 when male teachers were enlisted into the forces, evacuees from several cities arrived and equipment was in short supply.

In 1945 Eastwood Higher Council School became Eastwood County Secondary School and in 1947 the school leaving age was raised to 15. Difficulties with equipment and staffing continued for several years.

The school played a major role in the presentation of a pageant in Hall Park to celebrate the Festival of Britain in 1951. This included dramatic scenes portraying incidents from local history.

Mr. A. H. Scott retired in July 1953 and Mr. E.C.Williamson became the acting head teacher in September.

In November 1955 Mr. R.F. Cotes became the new head teacher. He introduced a new timetable and re-organized the classes. These now all became mixed and streamed in January 1954.

Staffing now increased to 21, discipline was strict and a uniform and competitive house system were encouraged.

Further curriculum development followed. Out of school activities included visits to local theatres, concerts and factories. Several clubs and societies were established and both national and continental visits made.

A social service scheme that involved the weekly visit to local elderly housebound people by several pupils was much appreciated.

In 1957 the school buildings were further extended using the 'Derwent Structural System.' These included 4 classrooms, a laboratory, 2 practical rooms, a gymnasium, dining hall and kitchen. Improvements were made to the sports field, and tennis courts were constructed. Continued success in sport, drama, and music was applauded at annual speech days.

A School Leaving Certificate was introduced in 1959 and in 1960 several pupils were entered for the new Certificate of Secondary Education.

In September 1972, after much consultation and planning, the Eastwood County Secondary School and Eastwood Hall Park Technical Grammer School were amalgamated to become Eastwood Comprehensive School.

Mr. B. R. Groome was appointed the headmaster.

The Walker Street buildings were demolished in 2005

Walker Street staff of 1955: Back Row: Mr. Burton: Miss Clarke: Mr. Martin: Mr. Wright: Mr. Chambers: Mr. Johnson: Miss Robertson: Mr. Thompson: Miss Edgington Miss?
Front Row: Mr. White: Mr. Phillips: Mrs. Longdon: Miss Williams: Mr. Cotes: Mr. Williamson: Miss Dove: Mr. Bakewell: Mr. Ross: Mr. Jackson.

D.B. CHAMBERS

....

Chapter 10: Remembering 'Owd Eastwood'

Joe Cooper and John Bowers welcomed our interest in their memories of 'Owd Estwood,' both started work at Allcock & Sisson's, (Builders and Joiners of Eastwood.) Between them both they chalked up 64 years with that company.

John Bowers, recalls that company owner Frank Sisson died aged75 and the company of Allcock and Sisson closed in 1984. They'd also been wheelwrights and coffin makers, using quality oak for burials and elm coffins for cremation, (elm because it was cheaper and for burning.)

John, who is now aged 85, was born in the Malt Rooms on Church Street and says that 'Butcher Noon' would collect the rents.

The family moved to South Street when he was still a baby and they lived there until he was 18 years old, then moved to Midland Rd.

He picks up the story in his own words: 'We used to be in a gang at Baily Grove end of South St. We spent most of our play time down at the two canals and the Erewash River. The canals were called Top Cut and Bottom Cut.

The Inkline Railway that went from Shipley Boat to Shipley Coppice Pit had two woods close by, known as Shipley and Cotmanhay Woods. We would have three crossing points on the Erewash River, beside the bridge on Lacy Fields: one was called Monkeys Ladder, one was known as Elephants Tusks and a third

point was High to Low Jump, which you could only do one way. We also used to play in an area between the two canals at the end near the Great Northern Inn. It used to be a tip in the 1920-30's. It was overgrown with everything and we called it the Bushes.

In winter, when the canal had ice on it, we preferred to slide and skate on what were the Filter Beds form the local sewerage works, and we called it the Muck Ponds. It was near Bailey Grove Laundry.

We also used to go into the park where White Hall Park School now stands. There was also 'Bobs Brook' at the bottom of the park

which fed Beggarley Baths and the canals at Langley Mill. This park was outcropped for coal in 1944-5. I fell in the canal three times!

We mostly went to the pictures on Saturday afternoons with our three pence pocket money. If we managed to get into the two pence rush, we would call at Glover Butchers and buy a half pence of Savoury Duck, about as big as your fist. It was a good meal.

Most of our school holidays were spent down the Erewash and the canals. I can remember the Rex Cinema being built and Birnam Products, and Shell House on Church Street.'

Harry Riley's note: John has compiled some old Eastwood terms and sayings from memory, and here is a small sample:

'Outa goin on' or 'Ow bista goin on.' - meaning Hello Friend.

'I arna bothered' - I am not really concerned.

'It's not woth tinkin abawt.' - Do not give it a thought.

'Tha muna goo.' - You should not go.

'Asta bin?'- Did you go?

'Yud nivera thowt it.'-You would never have thought it.

The hawker came around on his horse and cart about twice a week and would shout:

'Sharn't be rownd t'morra, apples a pand, pears same! His name was (Snaker) Bentley and his store was opposite the Moon and Stars Pub at new Eastwood.'

John says as kids they would call in at New Manley's Mill and purchase three penny worth of Cow Cake. He believes it was comprised of mainly grass, compressed into a meal cake for farm animals and that after a hard day's play it was a very satisfying snack.

Here are just a few of John Bower's old photographs...

Rear of Lord Raglan Pub. Newthorpe Common, 1913

Newthorpe & Greasley Railway Station

The old Tannery at Giltbrook, note the railway line and pond in the foreground

One bin and a *weekly collection!*

This dwelling was known locally as Shell House, Church Street

Modern looking trolley-bus on route to Nottingham, and just approaching the Midland Bank, Eastwood Town Centre.

The Sun Inn Eastwood. Early 20th century John Bower says 'Mad Harry's' stall was alongside the pub.

....

Remembering 'Birnam's'

By Keith and Beryl Brindley

Between them they'd worked at Birnam's a combined one hundred years, since 1951.

Keith says that being a fresh-faced and thin, fifteen year old lad, walking into a dark factory with other new starters, I was on edge, we were all given Clock-Cards with our identity numbers on. I found out later the man in the office was Les George. Talks of his interest in football soon became clear. I was told he instigated the formation of Eastwood Town Football Club. His hard work and hours spent soon had the team up and running and his ticket selling helped to raise funds.

The canteen, prepared by Mr. Frank Brown and his team of girls turned out good food, i,e, one penny for tea, two pence for a bacon or sausage cob. The lady helpers were Jean Brown, May Duffield and Mrs. Mann (pot-washer.)

Midland General Bus Company ran six coaches each working day to bringing workers from surrounding areas. A train also dropped off workers at the station adjacent to the factory.

The Clay family were involved in most of the work carried out. George (Senior Foreman) his wife Fanny on the mattress machines and son Roy and brother John (square link) Albert (ovens) Gordon (springs.) All the Clay family males were outstanding sportsmen.

Jack Winfield and his wife Beatie, too long-serving workers turned out all times of the day and night to clean up flood-water after heavy storms.

Before the advent of fork-lifts all coils of wire had to be moved by two wheel trolleys-Ruben Cathrine gathering speed past the first-aid to the trolley room.

The Transport Department comprised of: Frank Burton (manager.) Plus Ted Payne- (6 foot six inches tall.) Stan Clarke, and Les Parry (a spare-time wrestler who would always visit Ilkeston Fair, to enter the boxing booth for his yearly knock-out- this earned him a few shillings.)

Martin Wright (Tony) was a true ambassador for Birnam's, always well-dressed and always available to take employees to Sheffield (T.W.I.L- Tinsley Wire Ltd. H. Q.) for the company doctor/hospital, nothing being too much trouble.

Over the years, starting at Roker Park, many local footballers represented Birnams. Vic King, a one armed winger, must have been the fastest man over 50 metres. Trev, Smith, Dave Bagshaw, Spud Cater, George Gordon, Roy Clay, Mick Booth, Don Rowley, Jack Gunn, Fred May, Mick Grainger, Herbert Charlesworth (trainer.)

Nobody stayed down for long when Herbert was seen coming towards them.

Harold Straw and Clarence Hawkins held these teams together; the manager: Eric Best always gave every help when big matches were to be played.

Another point, over the years Birnam Employers have become Mayors of Eastwood: Fred Walters: Jack Wormall: Susan Bagshaw: Don Rowley; David Bagshaw.

Keith's Question: If any ex-employee meets Trev Smith or David Bagshaw, just ask them, what was your clock number? It would be a good bet they will remember it.

Keith and Beryl Brindley

Birnam's Players, with Keith Brindley standing, first from left.

....

Harry Riley's note:

Yet another large local employer now sadly long gone was Collaro Ltd. of Langley Mill. At one time this company had 4000 employees working day and night shifts.

Collaro Ltd. Langley Mill May 1944

....

Eastwood Lads Club, Scouts, Cubs and Lifeboys,
Boys Brigade, and Air Training Corps
By Mick Parkes

Throughout my formative years I lived on Grosvenor Road, behind the Rex cinema and George Hawksworth's Chip Shop. In fact, I lived at number 26 until I was 23. I was born in 1939 and started school in April 1944, at Devonshire Drive. The infant Headmistress was Miss Vosper and the upstairs Headmaster was Mr. Sprittlehouse; who seemed to rule with a rod of iron but was really a soft and kind gentleman.

In the early post-war years the majority of Eastwood lads had some sort of involvement with the Lads club on Church Street, and I was one of them, being a member from the age of eight until adult.

The club comprised of a large Victorian house, number 8 Church Street (where the Hartwell complex now stands) with two large wooden huts at the back,

and brick built storerooms known as 'the dens.' All members had to belong to one of the following organizations: Cubs, Scouts, Life Boys, Boys Brigade or Air Training Corps. Meetings took place in the huts whilst the house contained a library, snooker and table tennis rooms, canteen and chapel. First and foremost all organizations were based on discipline and self-respect with keen and healthy competitions between them all.

I joined the clubs and there met Barrie (Baz) Woodcock who became my great pal for 60 years until his death in 2011. At age 11 we graduated into the Scouts among the big boys who included Geoff Richards (my first patrol leader,) Pat Hamilton, Brian (Broody) Bostock, Ray Heathcote, The Machin Brothers and the Plant Brothers. What a lively, fun-loving set they were! Activities were very varied and included woodcraft: climbing: camping and night hiking. Summer meetings were often held at Beggarlee baths on Engine Lane. The open air baths had been dug out by members of the Training Corps in the late 1930's and provided many happy hours for all, but the Lad's club members enjoyed the reduced price of 2 pence (just below a new penny.) it was a case of 'first in, clear the frogs out!' Sporting activities within the club were wide and varied: many trophies were won for football and table tennis. They also staged a cricket match at the '1951 Festival of Britain Pageant.'

The drum and bugle band was second to none in the area. Many will remember Bill Holmes playing The Last Post and Reveille at the Cadets Cross for the annual Wakes Sunday Memorial Parade.

One of the main highlights was the prize-giving and display night at Walker Street School.

Junior members; after many weeks practice, did a precision marching display carrying lighted candles in jars. There were gymnastics, boxing and first-aid competitions, and many comedy stunts, before well-earned prizes were distributed.

The most exciting times had to be the camps at the sponsors (Dawson Chambers) farm at Wirksworth. Transport was by Graingers open-backed haulage lorry. All groups piled onto the back of the lorry, surrounded by the equipment and were waved off by a large crowd of parents. No one ever tried to stop 50 lads standing and grabbing hold of branches going up Longway Bank! 'By the late 1950's administration of the club was taken over by the Coal Industry Social Welfare Organization (CISWO.) The increase in commercialism and other, 'less demanding' interests for youth, forced the club to close in 1963, a sad event. Even so, all was not lost as the money from the sale of the premises was put into 'trust' to pay grants to local youth organizations. Health and Safety
weren't invented,

This continued for 50 years, and in 2013 the trust was wound up and all remaining money paid out to local youth groups.

I had the pleasure of being a trustee for some years until it's closure. never lost a lad! A little while before the Lad's Club closed a new Boy Scout Group was formed at Greasley by Arnold (Bunny) Eyre, with headquarters at the 'Old Spot' on Main Street, Newthorpe.

I joined them and was Scout Leader there until 1968, when a change of occupation and more distant work meant I could no longer afford the time to commit. I had many happy and rewarding times in the Boy Scouts, but often I ask myself if I could have kept up with the times and the many changes to Baden Powell's original vision. We shall never know, but it's nice to have these good memories.

Mick Parkes

*Local Youth Group recipients of the final distribution
of Eastwood training Corps trust Fund.
With the Trustees and Council Reps. Feb. 2014*

1st Eastwood Robin Hood Scout and Cub Group 1950/1

....

Arthur (Bud) Morris: Born March 1930 ...died Nov. 2003
(As remembered by his son Grenville: 'Young Bud' Morris.)

Sport was always to be a big part of Arthur (Bud) Morris's Life…football and cricket. Starting in the Boys Team at Giltbrook under Tommy Bird. He worked at G.R. Turners at Langley Mill and played football for the Butterley Company. Many games were played at the Mansfield Road Accademy Site, with the formation of Eastwood Town F.C. in the 1950's.

From then on he became a one-club man for the Badgers, in young Bud's own words 'putting him in the same class as the great Sir Bobby Charlton…a true sporting gentleman!'

In the late forties and early fifties, due to his outstanding ability at football and cricket, he played for many of the local teams: Birnham Products: G.B. Turners etc. He started his cricket at Shipley Boat, Alan Hunt having persuaded Bill Noon, owner of the pub, to mark out a cricket pitch at the rear of the Shipley Boat Inn.

Bud is front row, second from left. Birnham Products 1947

Eastwood – My Memories – I. A. (Arthur) Rowley

I was born in May 1942, a few doors away and two days after Jeff Astle who obviously was a good friend for many years, as were

our mothers.

Most of the time in my pre-school years was spent on the family

 farm, Newthorpe Lodge farm, situated down Billy Halls Lane, off Newthorpe Common, between the canals and the Erewash River.

Being a member of the Steeples family my mother worked on the farm and I spent a lot of time there and recall that my mother,

 borther and myself were responsible for delivering the milk door to door on a horse and cart using milk urns and measuring jugs.

When we had finished I was allowed to ride the horse (named Dick) back to the farm and into the paddock stables.

However when I was 4 or 5 years old my parents separated and my mother, sister, brother and I moved into a house on Queen Street

 (now Queens Road North.) This location proved ideal for me as I was nearer to Devonshire Drive School and more or less in the centre of the town. This meant that I could go and play on the 'Mowlems' and then walk down to new Eastwood and go

swimming, bird nesting or train spotting at Shipley Boat Station or whatever else the lads wanted to do. Conversely I could go down

to the 'Breach' to other friends and go to Beggarly Baths to swim or to Moorgreen Reservoir and bird nest. I remember on one

occasion four of us: Jeff Astle: Pete George: Colin Gilbourne and I being chased by the gamekeeper – unsuccessfully!

Staying closer to home we would play football and cricket on Queens Square or Devonshire Drive; telegraph Poles, pieces of

wood, tennis balls and jumpers being the requisite kit for both games. Sometimes, depending on the time of day we would

venture down to either Mansfield Road or Church Street recreation ground to play.

On leaving the infant school and passing the '11 Plus exam' I went to Henry Mellish Grammer School where I had to play Rugby and Cricket for the school but I still maintained contact with my local mates, mainly through sport and the Rex Cinema on Saturday Nights.

When I was thirteen years old I started playing football for The Lads Club, for Gordon Fletcher , and cricket for Eastwood St. Marys, for the Reverend Peter Caporn, when not cdommitted to the school sports.

On reflection we were very lucky to grow up in the late '40's and the '50's as it was safe to wanderand roam anywhere in the area without parents worrying, plus the fact that Eastwood was a 'true town' in so far as whether you lived on 'The Breach,' in 'The Buildings' or Addison Villas, everybody seemed to know or know of each other. This was all helped by most parents working in local industry (Coal Mining: Birnhams: Vic Hallams: Wolsey etc.) and their children went to Devonshire Drive and Walker Street Schools. This formed a close bond and Eastwood was very real community.

When I was sixteen years old the Vicar closed St. Marys C.C. and I moved to Eastwood Town C.C., as most of the players were friends.

A year or so later I played for E.T. F.C. Reserves and later I was playing for the first team at Basford United , as Right Winger.

From the age of seventeen I was playing every week for either E.T.F.C. or E.T.C.C. and this was to continue for about 13 years, playing for the cricket club for about 13 years and the football club for 17 years, with the latter taking preference as I was Captain from the age of twenty. According to some records I played about 850 games for the football club but what people don't realise is that I played in every position on the field, with one exception-Right Back.

My Sporting Life:

Cricket:

Eastwood St. Mary's + Eastwood Town, continued for 17 years.

1960 ; voted best young cricketer in Notts. –Joint Winner with Jeff Astle.

Football:

Devonshire Drive Infant School.

West Notts Boys.

Eastwood Lads Club- 4 years (Graham Machin Manager)

Notts N.A.B.C.X1.

Eastwood Town F.C. – 17 years Captain,

 (in 1962 when Geoff Goodall retired.)

Notts F.A. X1- eight seasons, Captain for seven.

England Amateur X1 Squad -1968.

The fondest memories I have are of the fabulous F.A. Amateur Cup years in the 1960's when we played teams like Bishop Auckland : Whitley Bay: Spennymoor: Penrith etc., from the North and Finchley: Enfield and Wealdstone from the South.

 All big clubs with a lot of money! We managed to reach the last sixteen in the country on 20 occasions, a massive achievement, and and became the best Amateur football team in the east Midlands.

The BBC even came over on our training night and filmed us going through our routines, conducted several interviews and we appeared on Friday Night in the local sports programme.

In those days we pulled in large crowds, several over 2000, one being 2,700

and the people of Eastwood and surrounding areas were proud of the club's achievements.

The commeraderie in those days amongst all the players was marvellous and I still socialise and maintain contact with a dozen or so players from that era , although this has its downside as Alan Brown, probably my closest and best friend from those days recently passed away; yet his step-son still maintains our connection and we occasionally meet for a drink.

Question?

How many players (or supporters) are left who remember playing on the original Corronation Park Football pitch?

ARTHUR ROWLEY 2016.

Arthur Rowley receiving a cheque for 'Best Amateur Player Of The Year, from Nottingham Evening Post Editor.

Arthur Rowley

Chapter 11 : Civic Duty and Assorted Subjects

Art:

The Parnham Gallery on Scargill Walk Eastwood is run by Malcolm Parnham. Malcolm was born at Nuthall in 1954 and he attended Larkfields Junior and then Kimberley Secondary School and finally Mansfield College of Arts. After various factory jobs he decided in 1986 to paint full time. He had various exhibitions all over England and in 1998 he opened his gallery at the Craft Centre on Scargill Walk where he specializes in local landscapes and steam engine scenes in both oil and watercolours. From his gallery he also runs a very successful 'oil painting for beginers class' several times a week.

The Parnham Gallery:at The Craft Workshops,
Note the famous 'D.H.Lawrence Blue Line
Pavement Trail.'
T: 01773 711112: e: mjparnham@aol.com

Example 1. Painting by Malcolm Parnham

Malcolm Parnham: Painting example 2

THE D.H.LAWRENCE BIRTHPLACE MUSEUM

8a Victoria Street: Eastwood: Nottinghamshire: NG16 3WA

T: 0115 917 3824

W: **www.dhlawrenceheritage.org**

Open: Tuesday-Saturday 10am-4pm

Booking advised: online or by phone.

Contact: Carolyn Melboune

This authentically recreated miner's cottage is the birthplace of world renowned Nottinghamshire author D.H.Lawrence. Visitors can experience the humble beginnings of the controversial writer who scandalised the literary establishment. Entry is through timed admission which includes a guided tour explaining the fascinating early life of Lawrence.

In each room there is meticulous attention to the style of the period, so that it really does transport the visitor back in time. From the Parlour to the Attic, everything appears just as it would have been in a Victorian household. A great experience for all, whether you are a Lawrence fan or not.

This charming, award-winning museum also includes an exhibition featuring pieces such as as his original water colour paintings and his headstone!

The museum is also your starting point to explore the beautiful surrounding countryside, which inspired so much of Lawrence's work, and The Blue Line Trail, an urban walk, taking you by other points of interest relating to Lawrence.

(Services: refreshments/ Gift Shop/ Translation Sheets/ Hearing Loop/ Group Tours)

D.H. Lawrence Birthplace Museum

The fire and cooking range inside the museum

The Art Group of Eastwood

The Dora Philips Hall on Wood Street is the home of the Art Group in Eastwood, which meets on Friday Mornings.

The Art Group was formed in 2003 by Maureen Lowe. Sadly in 2010 Maureen passed away, but the decision was made to keep the organisation going with several members volunteering to take on various duties to ensure the smooth running of the club.

Membership currently stands at approximately eighteen, a number which is limited to the amount of space available. Everyone works in whichever medium suits their artistic style, be it Watercolours: Acrylics: Pastels: Pen and Ink or Oils. There is always the

opportunity to learn and improve through taking advice from others within the group. Visiting experts are invited to share their knowledge and encourage everyone to try new methods, improve their technique and work outside their comfort zone.

Throughout the year there is a varied programme of activities, including exhibitions at local venues, an open morning displaying members work during the Eastwood Arts Festival and visits to various locations to paint local scenes.

In recent years members have visited Heage Windmill: the Cromford Canal: Beauvale Priory: Newstead Abbey: The Birmingham Museum and Art Gallery, and patchings Art Centre at Calverton. The group is a member of the Society for All Artists (the SAA) and a visit to The Society's headquarters in Newark has been arranged for later in 2016. It is hoped the Art Group of Eastwood will continue for many years to come.

The art group in action, practicing their skills

The Art Group of Eastwood

Writers:

Deborah Wardle was born in 1960. Her first memory was moving into 134 Church Street Eastwood, when she was just sixteen months old. The youngest child and only daughter of John and Dorothy Wardle, Deborah, with her two brothers: Philip and Ian, spent her childhood enjoying the countryside surrounding New Eastwood. Their immediate neighbours were Mr. and Mrs. Walker, whose farmhouse was attached to their home. Many childhood

hours were spent in their fields, which stretched as far as Langley Mill, along the train track, trains which often afforded them a family trip to Nottingham.

Deborah's father was born on Chapel Street, the second eldest of seven sons to Sam and Mary Wardle. Sam met her mother while both in their teens, after she moved to Eastwood from Nottingham during WW2. Her parents set up breeding and showing German Shepherd Dogs and a boarding kennel business during the 1970's in which Deborah was to take an avid part in their interest. She later went on to begin her own mobile hairdressing business in and around the locality, and due to her love of the countryside, she also qualified as a Forest Conservationist. Eventually moving away from her home town to reside in Cornwall. However, Eastwood

and its people never left her heart and eventually Deborah returned to live only a few houses away from where she was born.

It was then she began to write, putting her life experiences into words and the start of a very enjoyable career, with her third book hopefully to be released later in 2016.

Deborah Wardle and her books

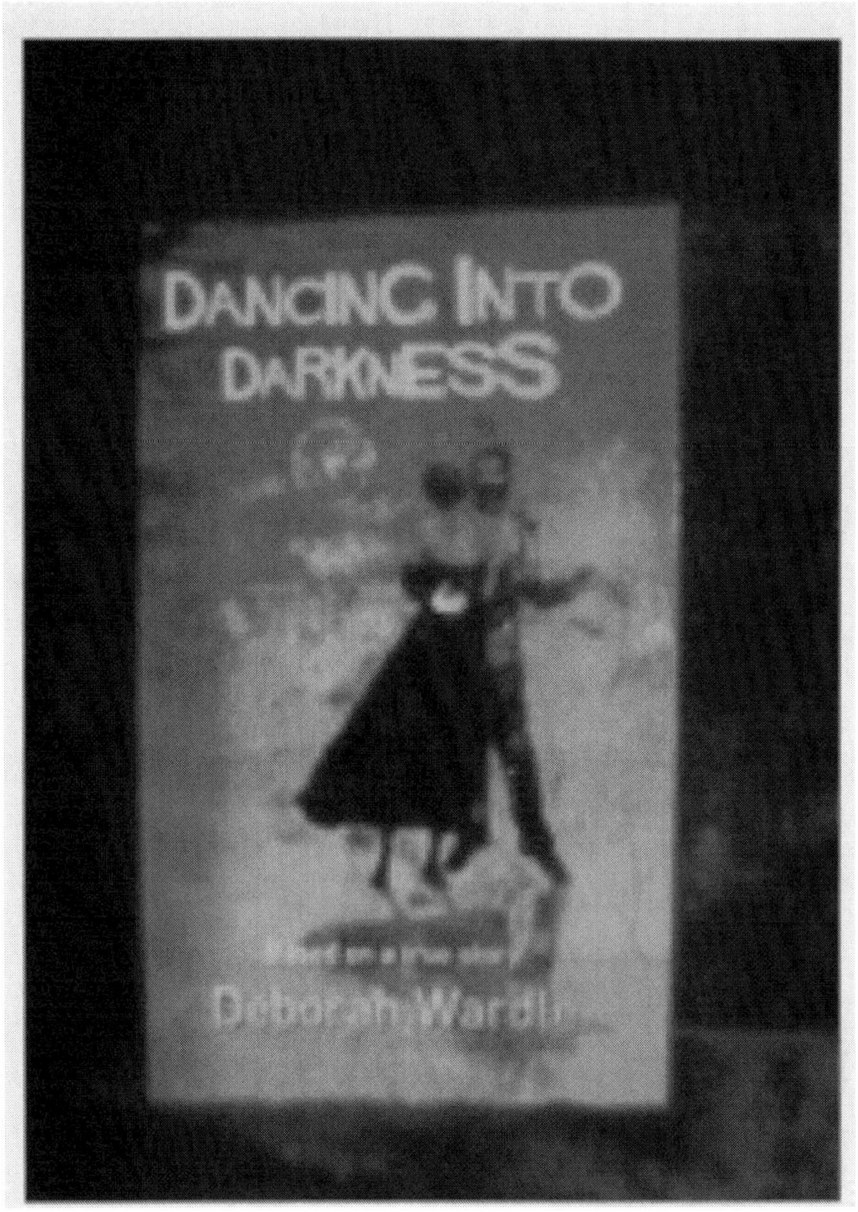
DANCING INTO
DARKNESS

Based on a true story

BEHIND THE LIPSTICK

DEBORAH WARDLE

My Mayoral Year in Office

By Eastwood's Councillor, Susan Bagshaw

I became Mayor of the Borough of Broxtowe in May 2015. There are 44 Councillors on Broxtowe Borough Council, and it is down to them to decide who the Mayor will be for the following year.

It is a great honour to be made Mayor, and a 'role' which I thoroughly enjoyed.

The engagements can be very diverse, i,e, one morning you can be visiting a Nursing Home for a 100th Birthday and later you could be attending a Nursery (both ends of the age scale.)

In your Mayoral Year you usually do around 400 engagements too, which is very time consuming, but a wonderful opportunity that you would only do once.

The role of the Mayor is non-political: you do not stand on any committee's to avoid any possible conflict that might arise. The role of the Mayor also involves you chairing the full council meetings, which can be very lengthy. After completing a year as Deputy Mayor I was elected to the position of the Honorable Mayor of Broxtowe and my husband became my Consort, although he referred to himself as The Male Escort.

But all in all, we get to see people who do work for the community, without any accolade and it's good to praise them for their contribution.

Councillor Susan Bagshaw

………………………………………………………………………………

Helen Sharp

My name is Helen Sharp. I was born in 1943 in Peel Street Hospital for Women in Nottingham, along with, I should think, 95% of all babies from the area. My formative years were spent in New Brinsley, and very happy they were too. A lot of my first memories of walking down Mansfield Road with a bag of chips in my hand from Gersher's at the top of the hill after a night at the Rex cinema with my Aunt Louie and Uncle Eric.

The old C5 Midland General Omnibuses never seemed to run to the times we needed them. Even the B3 or B6 that would have taken us to the bottom of Broad Lane didn't seem to smile kindly on us. Never mind we were country folk and walked everywhere so it came naturally. The MGO had a slogan: 'Whatever the weather we will never let you down,' and they didn't!

Once you got to Eastwood you could get anywhere. B1 would take you to into Mount St. Bus Station Nottingham. The A4 was a direct bus only, picking up at Langley Mill, Eastwood and Kimberley and then non-stop to Nottingham-they called it a limited stop bus.

You didn't really need to go any further. There was nothing you couldn't get in Eastwood in the '50's and '60's, it was a fabulous place to live then. I can remember most of the shops, especially the old Langley Mill and Aldecar Co-op, queuing up in Langley Mill for the divvy: two shillings and six pence in the pound was a lot of money. I knew when it was collected I would get my new anniversary dress for chapel. I seem to think this was the only brand new dress I had in any one year, which always came from Rowels of Heanor.

Growing up in and around Eastwood was great for teenagers. We had Milk Bars: Linwoods Music Shop: The Rex Cinema, not forgetting the Empire (we called the Flea-pit) plenty of places to buy make-up, dresses and shoes.

Most of my childhood was spent in Eastwood. There were plenty of fields to walk and play in, with the canal not far away…Paradise! Who could ask for more?

It was when my grand-children came along and I started to tell them about what they called the 'olden days,' that I realised just how much things had changed in such a short time. They didn't believe half of what I was telling them, so I decided to write it all down for posterity, if no one does, **it will be lost forever.** Now I find my generation love to be reminded of how happy and carefree times were then. Also I was very happy writing and remembering them myself.

'My Very own King.'

I couldn't believe my eyes. I was only eleven years old, that terrible age when everything was so much more dramatic. It was my lunch hour, I'd only been at the Matthew Holland School for a few weeks. It was so boring to be in the school grounds at lunch time, anyway, the weather was beautiful who wanted to be indoors? Not me! I'd not had time to make many friends so I'd taken to

exploring the surrounding area. Churchyards have always, and still do fascinate me. You can find a lot about the history of the area surrounding the church just by reading the different headstones. It was a bit difficult to read more than a few each day, which is just what I did. Unfortunately I started on the right side of St. Helen's (as you look at it from the road.) The usual 'babies gravestones' littered the ground and these always made me sad, as did the ones of the very old. I think the worst were the markers for a young mother and her baby. 'Likewise, born asleep.' The comfort came from seeing they had large families that had joined them and the fact they were not on their own down in the ground.

Months went by before I made it around to the left hand side and, there, not far from the church side door: the gravestone of Dan Boswell 'KING OF THE GYPSIES' in all it's glory, surrounded by a little iron fence. He was mine, all mine! A real live King, buried near my school, in a church which bore my name (St. Helens.)

Each day I would sit in front of his grave and read the inscription:

'I've lodged in many a town,
I've travelled many a year,
But death at length has brought me down,
To my last lodging here.'

I had been brought up all my life with gypsies. In fact the Smith family lived next door to my mother on Wharf Row in Brinsley and went to my village school. The family was large, but they were happy and well fed. They started the day off clean (which is more than can be said of all the children in my school.) They were the salt of the earth in more ways than one. They looked after the environment so well. They had to, it was their food; fuel, the very soul of their way of life. Without it they would not be able to live the way they did. I loved to listen to the stories they told of the wild animals and the places they had stayed in the year they'd been away from our village. I was so overawed by it all.

Here was I looking at the grave of their king. Me, a mere village girl. I sat day after day thinking, had I met any of his family?

Had they passed through my village?
Did he have a good life?
Was he a great leader of his people?
I could only sit and wonder.

This was something I never forgot, the impact has stayed with me forever. How often in life can you find a real 'King of your own,' and he belonged to me, and only me.

ೞೞೞ

Harry Riley's Footnote: **'My very own King'** *a true story, by Helen Sharp, is featured in the Gypsy Museum in Lincolnshire.*

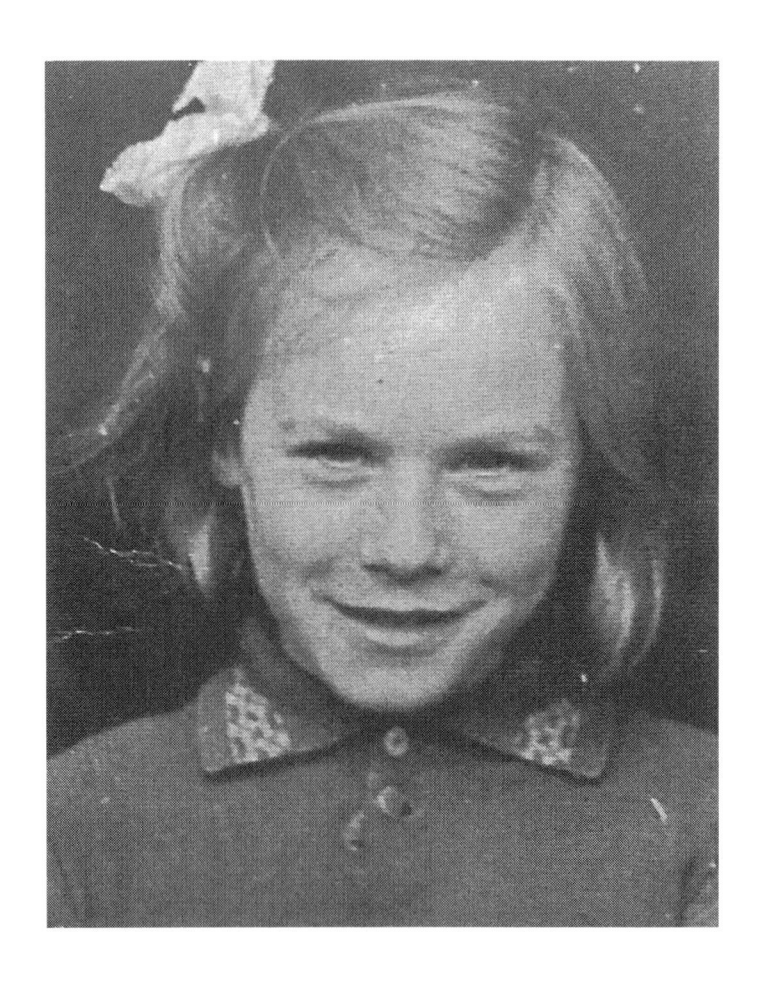

The young *Helen Sharp*

Helen Sharp 'en voyage'

Helen Receiving a book award from Mayor of Gedling

(This photo taken by Harry Riley)

My Story By Maria Kirk

I was born Maria Wyrobek, and as a baby my parents and I lived at the lock-keepers cottage on Langley Mill Canal, from there we moved to new Manleys Road, then on to the Breach, and I well remember going up Lyncroft and across the fields to Beauvale School, if the older children were in charge of us little ones they would take us across the fields (now Abbey Road) as long as the bull or cows were not in the field. If they were, it had to be the long way around.

Eventually we moved onto Nottingham Road, to the housewhich was two doors down from Smallers Garage. When we moved in, there was a little shopin the front garden, which my father had to demolish as it was a bit unsound. Apart from two years on Abbey road, I have lived at the same house since then.

I first became involved in collecting for the Poppy Appeal in 1970 with Colin Dyson, as organiser, he had the best pitch in Eastwood, and as Mr. and Mrs. Rawlings had the pitch outside the Co-op, I got the other end of Eastwood, but eventually moved up to the co-op. I joined the British Legion and was involved for many years on the committee as Poppy Appeal Organiser.

The question I was asked every year was: 'What made you get involved in Poppies?'

And the answer I gave and still is so: 'My parents!

It is my way of acknowledging what they and thousands like them went through during the second world war.

My father was Roman Wyrobeck, he was born in Czuchow in the region of Upper Silesia in the Polish border. In 1939-40, when it was obvious that war was inevitable he, together with his younger brother, and many other young men from the area, ran away and joined the Polish 2nd. Corps (which later was attached to the British Eighth Army under Monty (Lt. General Bernard L. Montgomery, later to become Field Marshal, Viscount Montgomery of Alamein) as staying in Poland would mean either being forced to join the German Army or fleeing to the East would mean the Communists.

Their journey would be neither safe nor easy, they would have to hitch lifts, hide on trains and walk, they would endure hunger, fear and exhaustion, but they finally made it and joined up with the Eighth Army. My father fought in North Africa, Tobruk, Rimini, Italy, and Monty Casino. He was awarded the Polish equivalent of The Victoria Cross: 'For Outstanding Bravery in the Field of Battle.'

He never spoke about this or any aspect of his life during the war years, it was only a few years ago that I found out about his achievements, when I decided to claim his war medals. Little did I know that my dad, who was a quiet, gentle man, was a war hero. Although I would love to delve deeper and learn more about his achievements, I respect the fact that he never said anything about those years.

He always carried a sadness in his heart for his younger brother, who lied about his age in joining up and was killed in action, and I am sure he blamed himself. In his few possessions from those years was a little religious picture, with a message from a girl called Maria, who he met in Italy, she must have been special for him to keep this picture. Who was she, I wonder? I often look at this card and wish I knew.

When he left his home and family he took nothing with him, so I have no pictures of my grandparents or my father as a child, just a few army photos, and after two trips to Poland to try and trace my ancestors, I only managed to find my grandparents graves.

After the war, dad and so many Polish Servicemen came to England, to make a new home, as the one they had left behind was under Communist rule: the freedom they had fought for, sadly was not theirs to enjoy. His journey to his new home of Eastwood had begun.

My mother was born in Skowyatyn, in Western Ukraine and her journey to Eastwood took a different route. Ukraine was under Communist rule and the people of Ukraine had already endured many years of oppression, including the enforced famine by Stalin, which had killed millions by starvation. When war began, mum and the family thought the life under German occupation would perhaps be easier than under the Russians. How wrong they were!

In 1939, they, along with thousands of others were rounded up, and the young and healthy were taken as forced labour: 'Ostarbeiters' to work in German factories and on German farms. Somehow, mum, my aunt, grandmother and my uncle's little boy, managed to keep together and ended up in Germany, working as 'forced labour' in a factory. She would sometimes talk about about those times, but then she would get upset and change the subject, she and my aunt would share their meagre rations with my grandmother and the little boy.

One night my grandmother died of starvation in the labour camp and mum told me they laid her out as best they could.

The next morning the lorries came for the dead, and my grandmother was thrown onto the lorry like a bag of rubbish, to be either buried in a mass grave or burnt with the rest of the bodies from that day.

Eventually the end of the war was approaching and mum recalled that one dayall the people in the camp were herded into some sort of large shed where they were locked in, and petrol was being poured around the shed, yhey were going to be burnt alive, when the British army arrived and they were liberated. She recalled often, the gentle kindness and respect of the British soldiers.

The war was over, and the people became displaced persons living in UN refugee camps. My mother had a choice: go back to her village in the Ukraine (that was a no-brainer!) she would be living under Communist rule: to stay in Germany or to come to England as a European Volunteer Worker EVW, she made the choice to come to England, while my aunt chose to stay in Germany and my uncle's son was sent to America. So the family was again torn apart, and mum's journey to Eastwood began.

So mum and dad, through different routes, arrived in England and eventually found themselves in Eastwood, and a place called 'the mushroom farm.' I think it was originally a detainment camp for POW's from the first world war, but later when I was a child it was called the mushroom farm, because that is what it became, owned by a Pole: Ted Bubass. Here life was very different. Dad, along with the other men, went to work clearing mines on the coast and then went either down't pit, or to a factory.

It was very hard at first, they did not speak the language, people made fun and called them names, and adjusting to an industrial area was a very big cultural shock, as the majority of them came from rural farming villages with no factories.

Slowly they tried to settle in knowing that sadly they would never be able to return to their homes, that they would not be able to even make contact with their families back home or go visit. Some had left their wives and children, never to see them again. All they had were memories and if they were lucky, a few torn photographs. As the months went by they made friends and married to start new lives.

Although they all settled down and worked hard, they still had Identity Cards and had to report to the police station once a week, and when I was born I had my own card and was entered on the card as 'Alien Baby' (must have been the nose!)

Mum came over with quite a few girls from Ukraine including Anna Gayer, Mrs. Butenko and many others whose names I forget, but I do remember Mrs. Swientoniewski, who made the most wonderful Doughnuts (she had been a prisoner in Siberia) and who I christened 'Mrs. Doughnut.'

Also I remember Mrs. Klementowski, who eventually settled on the Breach in the end house of the D. H. Lawrence row, kept chickens and was very houseproud. Mr. Klem had to dust himself down before he was allowed indoors.

So many memories of strange sounding names filled my childhood, with wonderful accents, customs and traditions, kind and generous people, who had suffered so much and lost so much and yet despite all that, were trying to make a go of things in this new country. Bruno Dominikowski, whose cookery skills are still remembered, Joe Bahlaj known as `Poly Joe' (he was actually Ukrainian) a short stocky man who could drink ten men under the table. His strength in fights in the pubs of Eastwood was legend, apparently he had his own cell in the police station, but a man of great kindness when anyone was in trouble.

Little Bobby Smelich, Joe Maslowski, Roman Ceizlik, Ludwig Dewieski (a very talented embroiderer) Mr. and Mrs. Topolewksi (who I used to call the Topos.)

Mrs. T. was a very skilled collector of mushrooms, hence very popular among the men who loved their mushrooms. There were so many, many more whose full names I have forgotten, but who I recall with great affection, and who were all part of my childhood.

All these gave an exotic flavour to the little town of Eastwood, they were treated with suspicion on their arrival, but with their charming ways, the men soon turned the ladies heads and many married Eastwood girls, and little Eastwood was never the same again.

It was quite funny to hear the locals try to pronounce the names, for years at school I was nicknamed: 'wire neck.' It was hard to remember that if it was 'ski' at the end of a name it was masculine and for feminine it was 'ska.' Often I got my ska's and ski's mixed up.

After mum and dad got married I was born in 1948. We lived in lodgings at various addresses until my dad made enough money to put a deposit on a house. Times were hard and growing up was extremely difficult because of the conflict between the two cultures, and sometimes I resented it. I just wanted to be like all the other kids at school, but as the years have gone I am very proud of my background and my roots. I have been to Poland and Ukraine many times, I speak both the languages and respect their cultures and traditions.

I always remember my father would always stand up for the National Anthem, and say: 'The King welcomed us to this country and gave us a home, so we should always be grateful.'

So to the memory of all of you, I raise a glass of Wisniowska (Polish Cherry Vodka) because you all went through so much, and you are all part of the history of this town, and deserve a mention. **'That is why I do the Poppy Appeal!'**

The Young Soldier: Maria's Father:

Roman Wyrobek

Roman Wyrobek: England 1947

Maria Kirk at the Eastwood War Memorial 2016

Maria Kirk with her father's distinguished war medals

A Snapshot of Childhood

By John Armstrong

I was born in Nottingham during the Second World War.

My dad was a toolmaker working on armaments for the Royal Ordnance Factory, having previously served as an engineer in the Merchant Navy. My mum worked at players Nottingham. We lived on a farm at Bagthorpe with my grandparents and my uncle and his wife.

My first memories are of the farm, the livestock, mostly poultry.

The Italian prisoners-of-war working at the farm, were awaiting repatriation and they made a fuss of me, calling me bambino. Our doctor was a Mr. Gladstone. He would visit us riding a bike, imagine that today? He often had his free-range-eggs in his basket. Eastwood was regarded as the main town with its banks and shops.

A trip on the C5 or B3 bus was an exciting experience.

My parents bought a home in Loscoe, where I attended the local school.

The Head was an austere spinster straight out of a Dicken's story. A big shock for a child used to freedom on the farm.

My memories are of a community largely revolving around the Ormande Colliery, the sound of the shift-end horn, the miners making their way home on Saturday nights, full of high spirits.

Rationing was still a part of life, but I don't remember feeling deprived. People belonged more to their community. We had Gala Days at the Miners Welfare with marching bands.

I proudly remember my mum out-sprinting everyone in the married women's race.

I joined the Wolf Cubs and sang in the St. Luke's Church Choir.

I would watch the locals fishing in the Loscoe Dam and early evening I sat watching Lawn Green Bowling, with frequent warnings to be quiet.

Our treat on Saturday was a trip to the local Heanor Empire Cinema, accompanied by other kids: one penny each way on the bus. Three pence to go in and then a penny mini-loaf from the shop near the bus stop.

The cinema was pandemonium as the more unruly kids, refusing to be quiet, would test the resolve of the manager, to be then dragged out by their ear.

It was all part of the entertainment. We watched Batman, Flash Gordon, and the Crazy Gang.

This is just a snapshot of memories and a long journey to today.

For those of us retired, a sadness, when we remember a post-war community revolving around the hard work and enterprise of the times.

The hosiery, the mining, the engineering…all too numerous to list, and all gone…leaving only the scars.

Yet life goes on and people adapt, doing the best they can. I still feel an affinity to this area, and after all those years in retirement, I myself now play bowls at our local Coronation Park.

I remember fondly, the miners having their roll-up on the welfare bowling green, smoking their pipes, simple pleasures, friendly banter.
John Armstrong: Greasley Miners Welfare Bowls Club.

....

Chapter 12: Keeping Eastwood's Businesses Growing

Warburtons Bakery Eastwood

'Since Warbrtons was established in 1876. We have always strived to offer quality products that can be enjoyed by all the family. Starting in a single shop in Bolton, today we are the biggest bakery brand in Britain, and we pride ourselves on being able to deliver over two million fresh products to shops every single day. Sitting in the heart of the country, our Eastwood Bakery plays an important part in helping us to reach our consumers with the products they love, and has been baking our products since 1994.

We have also enjoyed playing an active role in the Eastwood Community. As a fifth generation business, family values are at the heart of the company and our approach to responsibility is designed to help our people and the communities we work with.

Our School Visitors at the Eastwood site have helped over 2,500 children in the last year alone learn about the importance of food nutrition.

Looking ahead, we see ambition as being absolutely fundamental to our future success.

Continual innovation underpins our business model, whether it's delivering wheat-and gluten-free products for those who have intolerances, or developing new variants of our products.

We look forward to continue working with Eastwood as we grow the business, and we thank its people for the contribution they make to our company."

Jonathan Warburton

Warburtons
SUPER
TOASTIE
Warburtons
TOASTIE
Warburtons
MEDIUM

Gillotts Funeral Directors

'Generations of Service'

We can trace our origins in Eastwood back to 1867, when the Leivers family started the 'Star Livery Stables' in Victoria Street, Eastwood, next to what was to become the birthplace of the author DH Lawrence.

William Leivers, who started the business, hired out horse drawn hearses and carriages to 'Undertakers' covering a wide area. With the demise of horse drawn transport and the introduction of motor vehicles, the business was renamed 'Leiver's Garage.'

By the 1970's the business was owned by William's grandson Robert Leivers, known as Roy or Bob, and his wife Ada.

In 1971, Barry Hutsby, whose wife Elaine was Ada and Roy's niece, joined the business as a Partner with 'Uncle Roy'. In 1973, Roy died, and at Aunt Ada's request, Barry and Elaine continued the Partnership with her.

The business continued to supply hearses and limousines to funeral directors in Nottinghamshire and Derbyshire.

In 1974, Eastwood and District Funeral Service was established, and in 1983 moved to its present location on Nottingham Road, Eastwood.

Mrs. Ada Leivers died in 1990, leaving Barry and Elaine to carry on the business.

Over the years the business grew, opening funeral homes in Stapleford and Kimberley, and in 1992 merging with Gillotts Funeral Service, a long-standing family business in Heanor.

In 2015, all four of its funeral homes were united under a single name; Gillotts Funeral Directors.

This was done to create a uniform identity across all four funeral homes, to reflect the independent family nature of the business, and in preparation for the opening of the firm's fifth funeral home in Selston. The Eastwood premises remain the central point for the staff and vehicles which serve all five funeral homes.

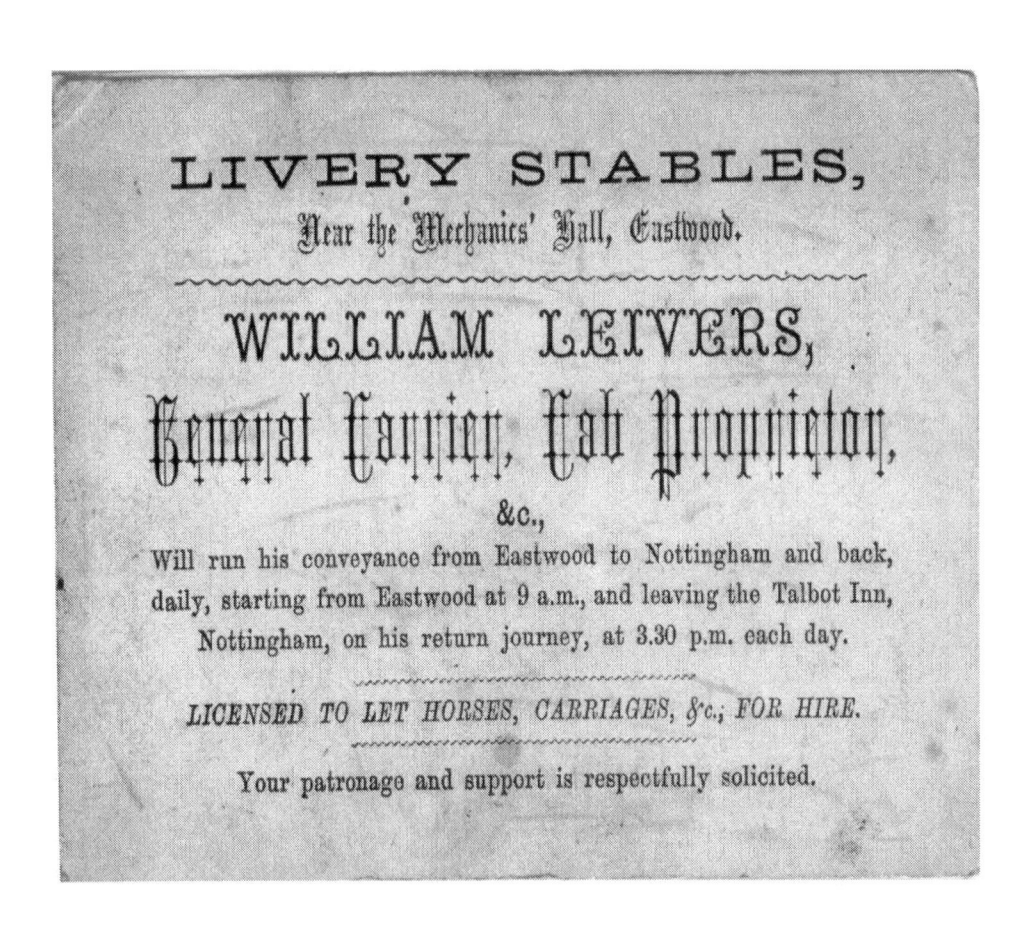

LIVERY STABLES,
Near the Mechanics' Hall, Eastwood.

WILLIAM LEIVERS,
General Carrier, Cab Proprietor,
&c.,

Will run his conveyance from Eastwood to Nottingham and back, daily, starting from Eastwood at 9 a.m., and leaving the Talbot Inn, Nottingham, on his return journey, at 3.30 p.m. each day.

LICENSED TO LET HORSES, CARRIAGES, &c.; FOR HIRE.

Your patronage and support is respectfully solicited.

"STAR" LIVERY STABLES,
VICTORIA STREET, EASTWOOD.

WILLIAM LEIVERS,
LICENSED TO LET

CABS, DOG CARTS, BREAKS, WAGGONETTES,
CARRIAGES, &c., on the most reasonable terms.

WEDDING AND **PLEASURE PARTIES**
ACCOMMODATED ON THE SHORTEST NOTICE.

FUNERAL CARRIAGES,
OF ALL KINDS, SUPPLIED TO ORDER.

AN OMNIBUS RUNS TO AND FROM THE RAILWAY STATIONS ON WEEK DAYS.
RAILWAY PARCELS RECEIVING OFFICE.

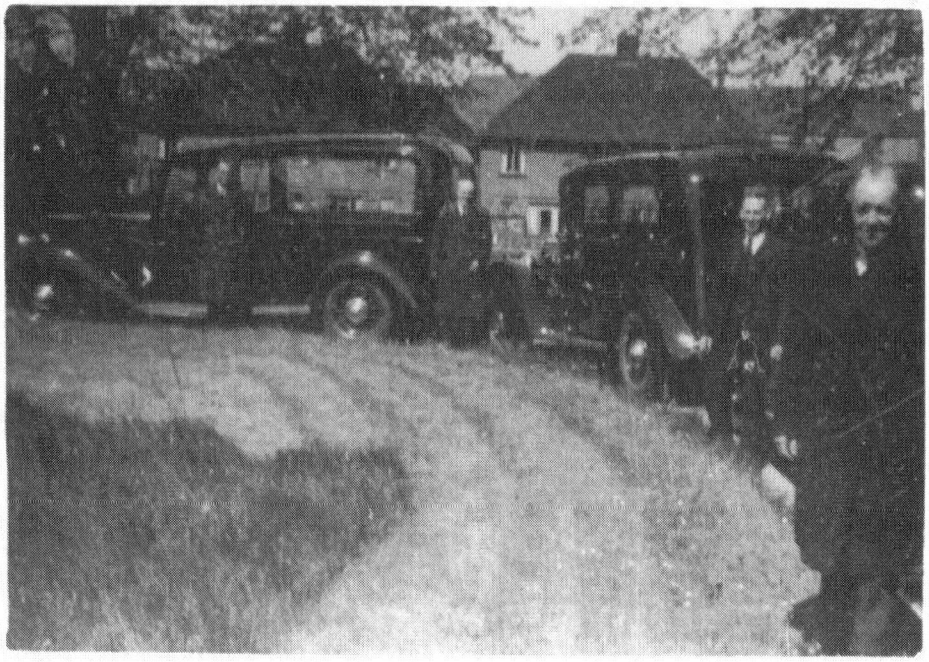

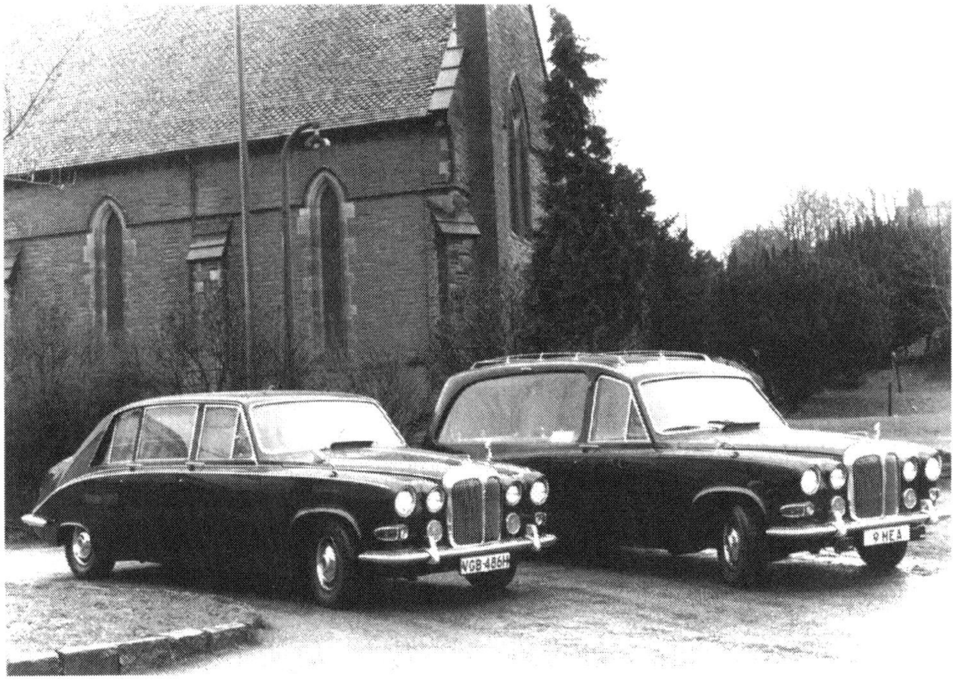
VGB 486H
9 HEA

Leivers Charabang

....

David Hammond Chartered Surveyors and Estate Agents

David Hammond Chartered Surveyors was established in the Lace Market in Nottingham in 1860. With increasing travel time demanded in order to get in and out of the City Centre to appointments, David Hammond looked around in 1999 for alternative premises from which to operate and which would provide ease of access to the M1 corridor and Nottingham's ring road system, together with ready access to centres such as Derby, Leicester, Mansfield and Alfreton.

Happily, premises were available on Nottingham Road, Eastwood,
and the firm purchased Nos: 9-11 Nottingham Road, a building which had, some years previously, operated as an estate agency but which had fallen into some disrepair.

An attractive late Victorian building, 9-11 Nottingham Road was Christened 'Churchill House' and was refurbished throughout with, amongst other works, offices being established on the first floor, Victorian fireplaces revealed and the front of the building cleaned and repointed.

The premises have allowed the firm to expand from a commercial agency, management and professional practice, to embrace residential estate agency and sales.

Eastwood's location with ease of access to major transport routes and East Midland's cities, enables the firm to continue its involvement with management, survey and valuation work throughout the East Midlands, more efficiently than would otherwise have been the case.

Karen Hammond.

Churchill House 9-11 Nottingham Road Eastwood

Our Times, Past and Present - Ian and Diane Johnson

Ian Johnson, wearing his 'Life Boy.' uniform.

Ian was born in 1949 and brought up in the Johnson family shop and home.

His Grandfather: Sam, married Ida Brown.

As time went on he retired and his son Nigel took over with his wife Doris.

The shop next door was purchased by Sam Johnson and he rented it out to a greengrocer about 1970-ish. The two shops were then knocked into one, In later life, and a few more alterations, a big store room was built and the upstairs turned back into two homes. Nigel passed away in 1979 and Ian and Doris ran the shop until Ian's wife Diane came into the business. We saw lots of different characters come and go at Hilltop and some lovely customers that had shopped with us for forty odd years.

Next door to our shop was the butchers: Fred West, in a lean-to the chemist.

The other side was run by Mr. (?) and his daughter. The shop had not changed in years. It was bought by Peter McDonald and upgraded.

Round the back of the shop was Allcock and Sisson- builders and Joiners.

Ian and Diane retired in 2010 and the new owners took over-The 'Singh-Rai' family.

Papers in days gone by came by train, they were often late and the paper-boys had to go to school, so it was all hands to the pumps to get them out.

271

Nigel and Doris Johnson

Chapter 13: More Important Memories

Age Concern Eastwood

(Colin Dyson)

During the early '50's, Colin Dyson decided 'a nice pop-in for a warm; a hot drink, and a chat' might be nice for our senior citizens of the area. The old Sunningdale building was a single-storey-prefabricated-building, and with the support of the local authority Colin was able to fulfill his dream. He hosted his little get-togethers for many years.

As a Councillor he later approached the Borough Council for alternative accommodation, feeling that the group had outgrown their current home. In 1971 he moved into 15 Edward Road, Eastwood, a building owned by the Borough Council that was originally a chapel.

There was a lot of work needed but over a period of years and many dedicated hours of commitment the building was eventually used for serving hot lunches and Colin had built up a group of volunteers who tirelessly helped to provide a community service.

In the early '90's Colin employed a paid Manager and things excelled, service improved and numbers increased. A legacy helped provide a new purpose built stainless steel kitchen. In 2000 and over a number of years a Trustee attained further funding which enabled much improvement to the building.

Sadly, Colin died in 2005 but not before being awarded the MBE for his community service, and the building was later named after him to become:

The Colin Dyson Centre. Another legacy in 2009 provided the scope to improve the 'small' rooms making them wheelchair accessible, along with a new floor to the main hall and re-upholstering of the armchairs.

A group of Trustees now employ four members of staff and continues to provide a much needed community service that strives and goes from strength to strength. There are over 70 members and around 100 meals served over the four days: Monday to Thursday. There is still a large group of volunteers; some that transport the isolated and lonely to and from the Centre; others meet and greet and look after the members with love, care and support. The smiles on our member's faces as they leave to go home makes everyone's efforts so worthwhile.

Eastwood Town Councillor: Mrs. Josie Marsters

Getting into party-mood at Eastwood Age concern

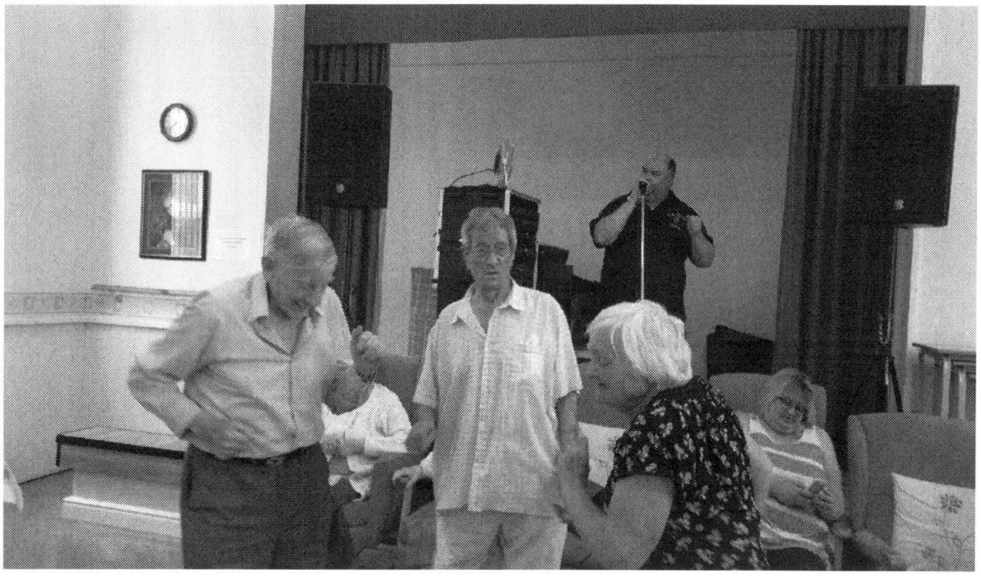

More entertainment at Eastwood Age Concern

....

Eastwood Conservative Club

Greasley Parish Councillor June Layton recalls her experiences of being at the Eastwood Conservative Club:

'It was a very happy time, although I was there mostly in a working capacity for many years.

I was secretary of the Y. C. as they were called then (young conservatives.) then I moved on to become secretary of Conservative Club where we had monthly meetings-organising speakers for political and social occasions.

The club was run by an elected committee with chairman, secretary and treasurer.

There was a steward and stewardess appointed by the committee to run the everyday workings of the club.

I organised notable business people of Eastwood to speak to us at meetings: Jim Menzies (Eastwood business man.): Lord Lanesborough.

Herbert Elliott (JP and President of the Eastwood Conservative Club.)

Lady Isobell Barnett-to name but a few.

When I was asked to write my memories of the Conservative Club I thought what a lovely idea-I felt honoured and priviledged to do so. Over the years I have met some lovely people and made friends with my connections with the club.

I also met my future husband at the Conservative Club.

Thank You.'

Councillor June Layton- nee June Baggaley.

Left to right: Lord Lanesborough: Councillor June Layton: Herbert Elliott (JP.): Jim Menzies.

Councillor June Layton: Herbert Elliott (J.P.):

Lady Isobell Barnet

....

Eastwood in the 1950's

By Mrs. F. E. Wharmby

'Not be long now' My Husband spoke loud enough to be only heard by me.

The bus had a number of people who seemed to know each other. As the bus travelled they had exchanged quickly spoken words, which to me sounded like a foreign language.

This was my first visit to Eastwood. I lived in West Bridgford on the other side of Nottingham.

'

'This is the library, ours is the next stop. Come on.'

I glanced quickly at a two story building with large windows: I had no time to answer: Donald was on his feet and making his way to the back of the bus. It gave a lurch as it halted beside a long row of shops.

As someone pushed rude fingers on my slender neck I was fortunate not to fall onto the pavement.

The lack of traffic made it easy to cross the road and we hurried to a narrow street that had a rusting street name: Victoria. We almost ran until we reached Princess Street and turned left. Houses built so closely together it seemed to my untrained eyes to be one long building.

'Here we are, up here. Stay close and don't touch the dog.' Donald moved into an alleyway with me as close to him as I could get.

The back door opened. I saw a scullery with a gas stove on legs, a brick washtub and a wide brown shallow stone sink.

Another door led us into a warm living room. This allowed me to see a heavily built woman who opened her arms in a wonderful welcome.

Donald's mother always gave me hugs and it was true love to us both during the future.

We were blessed with a daughter, Janet and during the following years we visited Eastwood and enjoyed shopping with Mama.

Eric Steeples. Family Butcher. We would pass Clifford's motorbike shop on one corner of Victoria Street. Sleath's Electrical Shop. This is where we stood looking in the window at the televised Queen's Coronation.

Mama and I sometimes went into the Co-op and bought family clothing. The Woman's Guild used to hold their meeitings in rooms above here.

As the years passed, shops closed, and some changed the goods for sale. Roads were built with traffic lights and horses pulling vehicles are now a rare sight in the town. Meetings for the public, such as the Eastwood Writers Group. The writers meet weekly, work is often published, and books written by local authors can be seen in the library. The Friendship Group in St. Mary's Church is still enjoyed by many of the town's young and older people.

The Rex Cinema, with it's beautiful art deco interior and the little sweet shop nearby were altered into a vast car park and a Safeway supermarket.

As time moved on this changed to a Morrison's supermarket.

Although I now live alone I feel blessed to be able to have my home in Eastwood. Friendships, which have lasted for years make me feel a happy person. A regular bus will take a person to the city of Nottingham or Derby. It's good to be able to say to a stranger, 'Oh, I live at Eastwood. Nice place.

A lot of history. Worth a visit.'

Mrs. F. E. Wharmby.

....

The Late Hazel Braithwaite

A tribute to Hazel:

I have been asked to write a few words about Hazel Braithwaite and I find it difficult to write just a few but I will try.

Firstly Hazel loved her family, she was proud of each of them and of their achievements. Hazel was a lovely lady who was loved by those who knew her. She had an intelligent, enquiring mind and she wasn't afraid to stand up for what she believed in, or to do things her way. She loved reading, followed fashion and loved to have a chat and a cuppa with friends, neighbours, and in later life, her carers. She loved animals, especially her cat.

Leaving school at 15, Hazel began working at 'Aristoc' at Langley Mill, later spending many years working at 'Wests Stores' in

Eastwood and also a few years as a doctor's receptionist at a local surgery.

Hazel was a staunch lifelong 'Labour' supporter, becoming a member of Eastwood Town Council and Mayor of the town for many years. She was an ex-Mayor of Broxtowe Borough Council and more recently made an Alderman. She worked hard and tirelessly for the people of Eastwood and was known by many.

The old Eastwood Town Council Chamber was very important to Mum, all were made very welcome there, and when an old gentleman from Japan, who wanted to pursue his interest in D. H. Lawrence, was found wandering around the park, he was taken to Mum's for tea and cakes, and then shown around Eastwood and the Council Chamber. He remained in contact until his death.

Our house was an open-house, the kettle was always on and advice and a cuppa available.

People were made welcome. Numerous visitors were entertained in the Eastwood Council Chamber, from here and across the world. A very special friend was Dr. Marilyn Gibson, an American Professor, who kept in touch over many years, and during a visit to Lerichi in Italy to represent Eastwood, whilst in office, Hazel met and stayed with the Mayor and his family. This I feel was very brave, as she went with no Italian, just her phrase book (this may have been an exchange visit, something to do with D. H. Lawrence, or some kind of celebration, I'm not too sure.)

Something else Mum greatly enjoyed was the planting of the 'Time Capsule'…there are really too many memories to list here.

Mum really enjoyed her year as Mayor of Broxtowe. We saw relatively little of her during that year, every day was busy and she travelled over 20,000 miles on 573 engagements. I have a folder full of 'Thank-You' letters from this time.

I have to mention my Dad at this point, Councillor Lew Braithwaite. He worked quietly in the background mainly, and without his devotion and unfailing support and interest, Mum could not have coped and enjoyed her journey in politics so much. He also spent many months designing the 'Eastwood Crest' which bears the motto: 'We Seek the Best'.

'Mum did so much, she is missed so much. She was my mum and my friend.'
Jill.

The late Councillor: Alderman Hazel Braithwaite

Councillor Braithwaite at one of her important functions

The new Eastwood Crest, designed by Councillor Lew Braithwaite and bearing the Motto: 'We Seek The Best.'

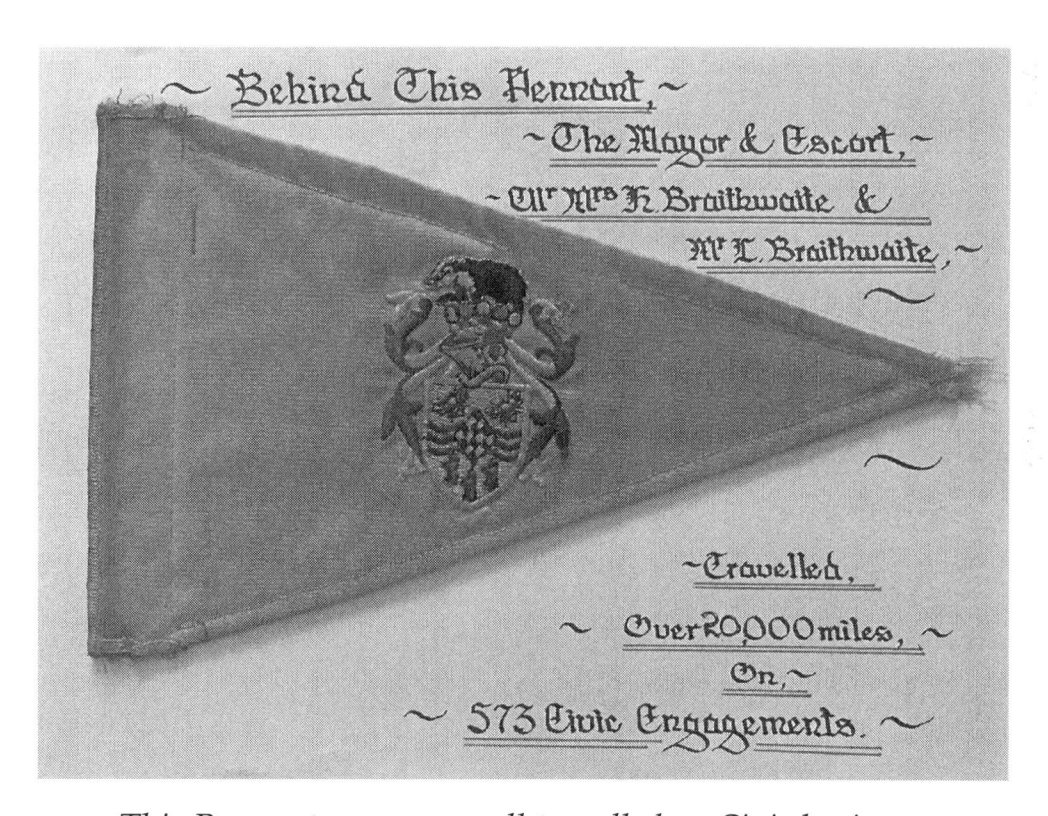

This Pennant was very well travelled on Civic business.

The Presentation of Eastwood's new Crest at a civic reception.

Doreen Lockett Remembers:

'When I commenced my banking career I was the junior clerk at Barclays in Eastwood. Mr. George Noon was the manager. He lived at Greasley Castle Farm. I remember the business and people of the town in the 1960's. There was J. H. Skelton: the chemist, Bricknell and Williamson: high class grocers, F. R. Chambers Ltd: wine and spirit merchants, selling Dale Abbey Sherry and Rookery Port, Manners Brick Company, Miss M. Waterall; ladies fashions, The Rex Cinema, Dr. Gladstone and many more.

Banking was very different then. It was all mental arithmetic, no computers or calculators.

The ledgers were handwritten and customers received their paid cheques with the statement. I would not have believed that after my retirement I would be using that mental arithmetic to do the bookkeeping at Greasley Castle Farm. George Noon had passed away and his brother James asked me to write some cheques etc.

One of my favourite duties was to don my Wellingtons and go down to the farmyard to draw the calves for their pedigree information. I would send the cards off to the Freisian Society and receive from them the pedigree to file away. Each cow was named and the herd was built by James Noon from the 1950's.

My time there was such a change from office work, being a part of the lovely Greasley countryside. Next to the farm is St. Mary's Church, which I attend. As the Church Guide I enjoy sharing the history and life of that ancient place of worship. I enjoy living in Newthorpe Village and sharing with local residents their memories of past life here.

Doreen Lockett 2016.

Doreen Lockett dressed in Victorian Costume, outside Barclays Bank Eastwood.

St. Mary's Church Greasley

George Noon of Greasley Castle Farm.

Interior of Greasley Parish Church of St. Mary.

Traditional horse-drawn hearse pulled up at St. Mary's Greasley

There are some remarkable people buried in St. Mary's Graveyard. Not least amongst them is that of Dr. Benjamin Drawater and his wife Dorothy. There is a plaque to the memory of the good Eastwood doctor beside his tomb, stating that he served as surgeon on a voyage of discovery with the famous circumnavigator Captain Cook. The plate states that he was a pious and good Christian. He lived respected and died lamented. He suddenly departed this life aged 68 on the 2nd. June 1815.

"UNDERNEATH
LIES INTERRED THE MORTAL REMAINS OF
BENJ. DRAWWATER, GENTLEMAN OF
MANSFIELD, LATE OF EASTWOOD
WHO SUDDENLY DEPARTED THIS LIFE ON
THE 2ND. OF JUNE 1815, IN THE
68TH YEAR OF HIS AGE.
IN HIS PROFESSIONAL DUTY HE HAD
ACCOMPANIED THE GREAT CIRCUMNAVIGATOR,
COOK IN THE YEARS 1772 – 1775.
HIS VIRTUES WERE COMMENDABLE
AND EXEMPLARY AND WERE HIGHLY
ESTEEMED BY FRIENDS AND RELATIONS
AND HIS SURVIVING FAMILY.
HE WAS A PIOUS AND GOOD CHRISTIAN.
HE LIVED RESPECTED AND DIED
LAMENTED."
FUNDED BY   1991
THE EREWASH COUNTRYSIDE VOLUNTEERS

Metal plate displayed beside the tomb of Dr. Drawater. In Saint Mary's Churchyard Greasley.

Another plate beside Dr. Drawater's tomb shows the voyages of Captain Cook.

The Screen of Remembrance

The chancel screen in loving memory
Tells a story of the true and brave,
Who in the war, to end all wars
For their country – lives they gave.

Never more to walk these fields
Or breathe again the Greasley air,
Instead they died on foreign fields
Where the poppies grow so fair.

From different ranks in regiments
Listed on the screen I see –
A Major, Corporals, Captains, Sergeants
Gunners, Privates and cavalry.

They were fathers, husbands, brothers,
Sons and uncles – neighbours too
Leaving all for King and Country
Achieving peace for me and you.

We all owe a great debt to them,
So read these names as you pass by –
Offer a prayer in grateful thanks,
AND MAY THEIR MEMORY NEVER DIE.

Doreen Lockett - May 2014

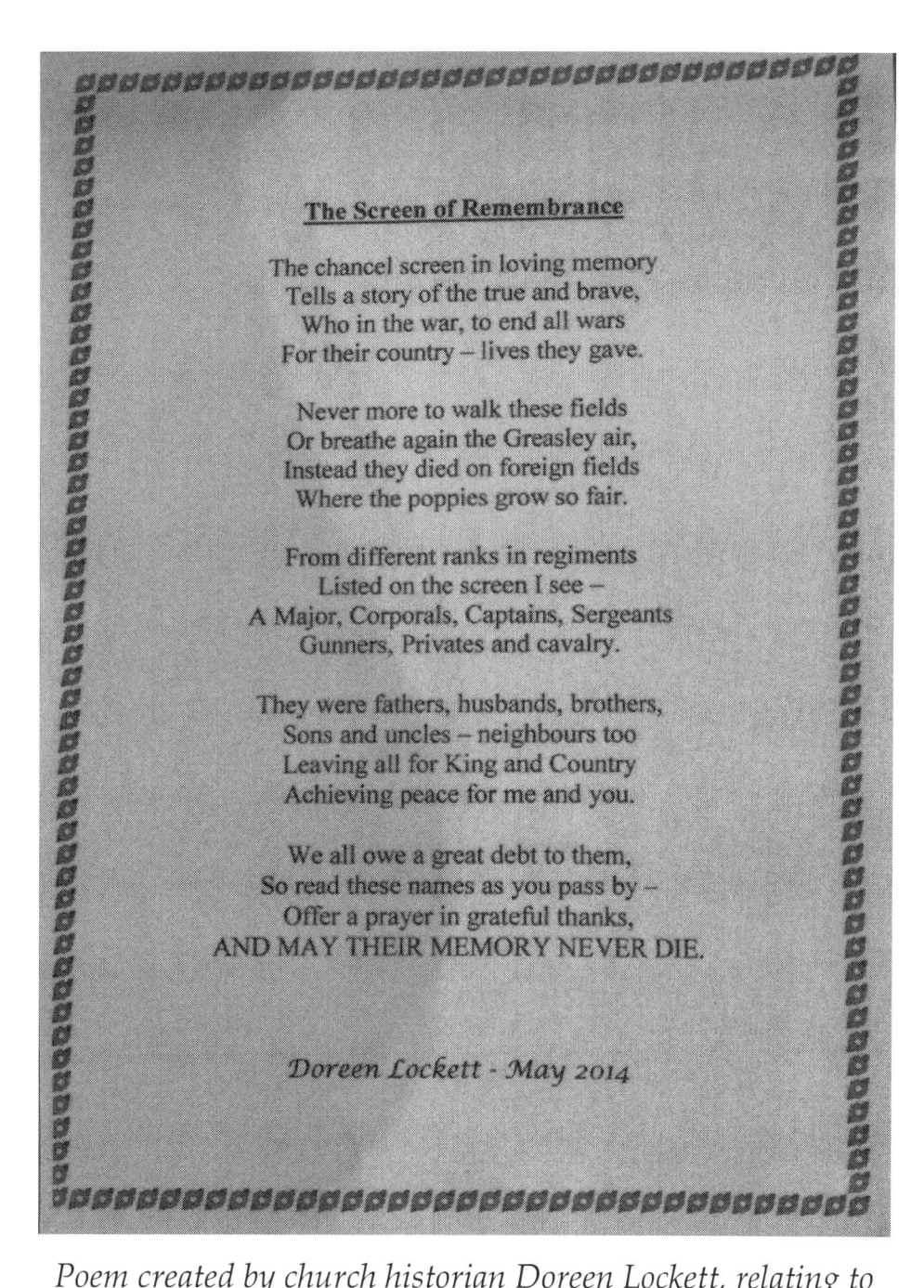

Poem created by church historian Doreen Lockett, relating to the church 'Screen of Remembrance' inside St. Mary's Greasley, and reminding us all that a list of names to those who gave their lives in war, deserves much more than a moments pause.

....

80th Celebration Eastwood Infant School

(A brief history of the school from Miss Sims to Mrs. Morgan Written by Kathleen Butler

By 1900 there were three schools in Eastwood. The National School administered by the church on Church Walk erected in 1863, a British School established in 1874 and installed in premises on Albert Street and an undenominational school opened in New Eastwood in 1899.

During the years 1808-9 the County Council took control of the three schools. The boys on Church Walk were transferred to the Albert Street School and the infants there were brought to Church Walk. In 1910 this building was opened to house the girls and infants. In 1932 the Albert Street School closed and the Juniors transferred here.

These buildings were occupied on 23rd May 1910. Miss Florence Sims was appointed Head Teacher of the infants with Miss grainger appointed head of the girls school. Her sister was Head of Beauvale. On 23rd May Miss Sims writes 'The school opened in the new building. Number on the books: 266.'

Looking over the history of the building it can be seen how it stood through three coronations, two world wars and the consequences of major events are seen from the entries in the log books. Our history shows how great changes have taken place in the life of our community and yet how many things do not change.

In the early days the school was closely run by Managers who visited the school regularly. Amongst our most noteable benefactors and overseers were William Hopkin and Major Barber.

On 24th May 1910 the second day we opened was Empire Day, an important event in those days. Miss Sims writes: 'May 24th May Empire day. Morning devoted to Empire Lessons, half day holiday in the afternoon.

Of our first Head Teacher, we learn that she was a very smart lady who paid very great attention to detail. She was always to be seen wearing a long black apron with two big pockets. `She had very strong beliefs inspired by her 'Montessory' training which encouraged children to work in groups. She attempted to enable all her 'pupil-teachers' to follow.

Today we think of In-Service Days as new, but not so, on 24th June 1910 the school was closed to allow staff to visit the 'Nature Exhibition.' The following month the school was officially recognised by the Board of Education and it was scheduled to accommodate 340 infants.

On September 6th 1910 the school was closed for the Moorgreen Show. The following day we were visited by an Inspector. He wrote: 'The school is making a very fair start but the teachers have much to learn before they can get into true and sympathetic touch with their pupils and can keep the children bright and interested and the lessons really interesting. Most of them have worked under considerable difficulties in the past, but the new premises are <u>all that can be desired.</u> And that what is needed now is that the staff should be given every opportunity in the near future of watching the methods of first-rate Infant Schools.

The school ought then to develop into a very good one.

William Hopkin reported in December of the same year that: 'the children are quite happy, a pleasant temperature probably contributing to this.

War came in 1914 and the horrific epidemics of 'Flu' which abounded in the following years.

In September 1914 a family of Belgian refugees were admitted. There were frequent absences due to 'Flu' and Scarlet Fever. In that time contact with Scarlet Fever necessitated quarantine and Miss Bowes, a member of staff, had to be absent for one month.

In May 1915 we had a treat. Some children were taken to Nottingham to see the soldiers marching.

School dinners were tried during the war. They were served at 3d, one and a half pence each 'to save bread.'

Miss Sims was not of the ordinary kind of Head for that time. She held an open afternoon in July 1917 where parents were invited to see the work and to have 'many conversations with the staff.'

War ended in 1918 and we had a halfday holiday to celebrate. We celebrated again in 1937. A Mrs. Butler came to school to distribute Coronation Mugs and we were awarded three days holiday for Coronation Celebrations.

Miss Sims left in December 1940 after 30 years service. She was succeeded by Miss B. Vosper. We were again at war.

During the following years the children and staff were party to the horrors of war. Children were fitted with gas masks through the school and were trained in what to do should we be bombed.

Miss Vosper tells us that an alert sounded and the children went home or scattered to their billets. Most of them returned when the all-clear sounded!

Dr. Kean conducted the medicals in February 1941 and found that the list of children suffering from malnutrition 'was much lengthened.'

Our numbers swelled due to the fact that the New Eastwood School was burnt down on 13th November 1944 and we had a large number of evacuees. Our numbers reached 293. In 1947 we had our own fire when the clinic was slightly damaged.

The school continued under the care of Miss Vosper who retired having served 20 years until January 1960 when Mrs. I. M. O'Brien took up the position of Head Teacher. By then our numbers were down to 149.

During Mrs. O'Brien's time we saw the introduction of Television and there were considerable additions to the buildings, toilets and staffroom.

The use of tape recorders and record players was introduced.

Mrs. O'Brien was a person who always put the children first. She took pains to know each child.

In 1980 Miss. A. J. Stewart took up the position of Head Teacher. In the early eighties our numbers fell. To make positive use of this the school was able to offer facilities for toddlers and pre-school children and also have available a resource room. During the '80's we have had more 'Head Teachers' than in all our previous history.

In 1988 Mrs. Day (Miss Stewart) left to become an Inspector and Mrs. Morgan took up office.

During the '90's we look forward to expansion and the provision of a nursery in the classroom now known as Area 7.

I would like to dedicate this booklet to all pupils and staff, past and Present.

K. T. Butler.

80th CELEBRATION

EASTWOOD INFANT SCHOOL

From Miss Sims to Mrs. Morgan
A brief history of the school
by Kathleen Butler.

Front row: Mrs. S. Shipman: Mrs. P. Ward: Head Teacher-Mrs. V.A. Morgan: Mrs. C. Mander.

Second Row: Miss Quinton: Mrs. Darby: Miss Bell: Mrs. Butler

Eastwood Infant May Day Festival 1954:

Eastwood Infant School Presentation: teachers: adoring pupils, flowers and a cake for the lucky lady

Kathleen T. Butler

Kathleen Butler has also published a brief history of our Lady of Good Counsel Hilltop Eastwood.

This is a beautifully printed booklet setting out the history of this Catholic Church in our midst, from the Parish's deeply rooted past.

It is a 'Must read' for anyone interested in Eastwood and Ilkeston, and the lords It was Lord Nicholas de Cantilupe who founded Beauvale Priory in the 14th

century and this history of Greasley and Beauvale and the Carthusian Monastry of Beauvale Priory traces the path of Catholism to the present day, including the veneration of our two patron saints: Robert Lawrence and John Houghton, martyred Priors of Beauvale: 4th May 1535.

There is now an annual pilgrimeage from Our Lady of Good Counsel to The ruined Priory and the story of the martyrs was told in a recent community play called 'The Cries of Silent Men.'

Our Lady of Good Counsel Eastwood

A Brief History

by

Kathleen T. Butler

BEAUVALE PRIORY
ST JOHN HOUGHTON
ST ROBERT LAWRENCE
MARTYRED
4 MAY 1535
PRIORS OF BEAUVALE
MARTYRS OF
ENGLAND AND WALES

Hilltop Children after weekday instruction at church

(before the Priory School was built.)

Hilltop Parents at the House of Commons, Westminster.

Chapter 14: Healthier Living

Breathe Easy Nottingham West

Left to right: Dr.Lim: Teresa Burgoyne and Nursing Colleague

BREATHE EASY NOTTINGHAM WEST

The Nottingham West group is just one of more than 230 across the country which are all part of the British Lung Foundation's support network. The BLF is the only UK charity working on behalf of all those with lung disease. We have been running for over 7 years now in Eastwood.

We offer support, advice, information on living with and self managing a lung condition. It is also a chance to meet and socialise with people in a similar situation. The group is open to all those who fight for breath, their families and carers as a result of a lung condition Just come along and join a really friendly fun group. We have a lunch club to start the monthly meeting, and a variety of medical, social and local interest talks. We also hold local fund raising events and raise awareness throughout the year.

Meetings are held on the 2nd Wednesday of the month 1.30pm – 3.30pm at the Catholic Church hall, Hill Top, 280, Nottingham Road, Eastwood, NG16 2AQ

Breathe Easy Nottingham West's also hold a twice weekly specially adapted respiratory exercise classes to help control breathlessness, boost confidence levels and well-being. Classes are seated or standing held at different levels depending on ability at Plumptre Hall, Church Street, Eastwood on Tuesday and Thursday's 11-12 All Welcome

If you wish to know more about Breathe Easy Nottingham West please contact Jane Reeve 07516 493459 or Teresa Burgoyne 07809 430616 If you wish to know more about the British Lung Foundation, Website : http://www.lunguk.org or phone the BLF Helpline: 03000 030 555

Please see our video on youtube

'Breathless Breathe Easy'

If you need Pulmonary Rehab they will accept referrals from local clinicians for adult patients that are registered with a GP within the Nottingham West Clinical Commissioning Group (CCG). The service primarily sees adult patients with a long term breathing problem. The patient will be seen by a member of our respiratory specialist team who maybe a physiotherapist or nurse.

The service can be contacted by telephone on: 0800 028 3338

Mon-Fri 09.00am to 5.00pm

TAKE THE NEW BREATHETEST visit breathtest.blf.org.uk

Teresa Burgoyne

Raising money at the BLF Big Breakfast at Lady Chatterley in Eastwood

Raising awareness of the BLF Breath Test with local COPD nurse Sonia for Breathe Easy week at Eastwood B&Q

Lynn, Colin, Rosie and Amanda at our 7th Birthday celebrations

Group photo with Penny Wood CEO BLF and Dr Lim local GP who were our special visitors recently to Breathe Easy Nottingham West

....

Brian Fretwell Bio

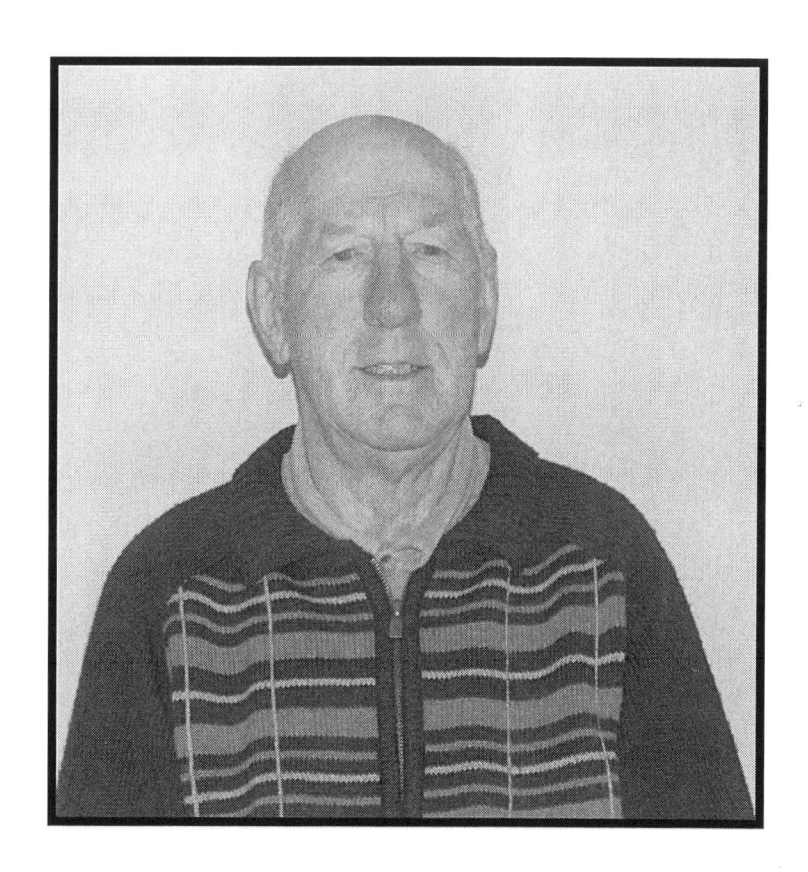

Brian was born at Eastwood and traded as a grocer in the Town for forty years. He is married with one grown up son and is deeply involved in community affairs, especially with the health and well-being of the elderly. He is a volunteer with both Eastwood Age Concern and The Eastwood Volunteer Bureau.

Brian has been Chairman of Eastwood Chapter & Verse Community Group since its formation and he still makes regular weekly visits to Eastwood Care

Homes.

He helps the annual British Legion Poppy Appeal. Although not a councillor himself, Brian attends most meetings of the Eastwood Council.

………………………………………………………………………………
………..

Acknowledgements

We would like to thank iT2 of Mansfield Road Eastwood:

http://www.it2group.com, for generously assisting with technical computer advice and donating copy paper and photocopying ink, without which we would not have been able to carry out so much of this necessary research.

iT2 Premises Mansfield Road Eastwood

....

Special Thanks go to Joy Melbourne of Eastwood Chapter & Verse Community Group who has selflessly given up her valuable time to accompany Brian Fretwell on his many visits to contributors homes, to help and encourage their participation in our work.

It is no mean feat for people, unaccustomed to writing a 250 word + bio of their life and family interests and community activities, to sit down and summarise their own involvement. But it is for future generations to witness and learn of the lives that were lived: the peoples' lives they touched and of their town's commitment to the veneration of the community at large.

Our Chapter and Verse Researchers; Joy Melbourne and Brian Fretwell pictured at the Eastwood Boxing Club open Day event.

We would like to express our immense gratitude to all who have kindly contributed to this 2nd. Volume and to ask those who, for whatever reason, may feel left out, to please bear with us, and to contact, and make sure you are represented in volume 3 for 2017.

Feedback is a very important part of any publication and especially so when, in order to keep production and purchase costs to a bare minimum, the editing is of a self-publishing variety.

Brian Fretwell and Harry Riley

Harry Riley Bio

I'm Harry Riley, Nottingham born author of murder-mystery novels, short story collections, town guides, local history and poetry. The photo above was taken in Northumberland on the banks of the River Tweed, close to where I once owned a small cottage and where I'd planned to retire. However, that's another story.

I've been married for over half a century, with two grown up children and one grand daughter. I enjoy reading the classics and my favourite author is Thomas Hardy. I broadcast a two hour nostalgia show each weekend on Kingsmill Hospital's Millside Radio: http://www.millsideradio.co.uk, and recently recorded a drama play with The Millside Players, taken from one of my short stories.

My books are available from Amazon:
https://www.amazon.co.uk/Harry-Riley/e/B005HXJRZ4
as both paperbacks and ebooks for Kindle

Printed in Poland
by Amazon Fulfillment
Poland Sp. z o.o., Wrocław